Collins
English for Business

READING
Anna Osborn

Collins

HarperCollins Publishers
77-85 Fulham Palace Road
London W6 8JB

First edition 2012

Reprint 10 9 8 7 6 5 4 3 2 1 0

© HarperCollins Publishers 2012

ISBN 978–0–00–746943–7

Collins® is a registered trademark of HarperCollins
Publishers Limited

www.collinselt.com

A catalogue record for this book is available from
the British Library

Typeset in India by Aptara

Printed in China by South China Printing Co.

About the author

Following a degree in Modern Languages at the University of Oxford, **Anna Osborn** worked in publishing as a Managing Editor during the 1990s. She retrained to become an English language teacher in 2000 and has since worked across Europe teaching students of all levels and ages. In addition, she has written a wide variety of English language learning materials including business and general study books, online self-study courses, and classroom workshops. Her most recent books are *English for Business: Speaking* (Collins, 2011) and *English for Life: Reading* (Collins, 2012).

ACKNOWLEDGEMENTS

The publisher and author wish to thank the following rights holders for the use of copyright material:

Page 61

The rich get rich, the poor get poorer? That could kill capitalism by David Robertson

The Times / NI Syndication (28.01.2012)

Page 69

How to live like the idle rich by Mark Atherton

The Times / NI Syndication (28.01.2012)

Pages 72–73

U.S. stocks drop as Greece struggles for accord by Kate Gibson

Reprinted with permission of MarketWatch, Copyright © 2012 Dow Jones & Company, Inc. All rights Reserved Worldwide (6.02.2012)

Page 77

Heritage, Culture and What the Japanese Can Teach Us About Business Longevity (extract) by Danny Brown (11.01.2012)

http://dannybrown.me/2012/01/11/japanese-business-success/

Page 81

The Leadership Engine by Noel M. Tichy

Copyright © 1997 by Noel M.Tichy. Reprinted by permission of HarperCollins Publishers

If any copyright holders have been omitted, please contact the publishers who will make the necessary arrangements at the first opportunity.

Contents

Introduction

Collins English for Business: Reading will help you to improve how you read business texts.
You can use *Reading*:

- as a self-study course
- as a supplementary material on a business communication or business English course.

This book includes a wide variety of types of text including business reports, schedules and budgets, social media, and business media. Many of the reading texts are authentic or based on authentic sources. You will find a list of the sources we have used at the front of the book on page iv.

Reading consists of 20 units, divided into four sections:
- Section 1 Emails
- Section 2 Doing business
- Section 3 Marketing and advertising
- Section 4 Business media and books

Unit structure

For ease of use, each unit follows a similar structure. It is recommended that you follow the order of exercises when working through a unit.

How to read – contains advice on the best reading approach for the text type.

Getting started – contains first reading activities that give you the opportunity to familiarize yourself with the content of the text before you start looking at it in detail.

Understanding – helps you to check your comprehension of the text.

Developing your reading skills – practises one or more types of reading skills which are most relevant to the type of text.

Language focus – highlights and practises useful language from the text.

Review – provides a conclusion to the topic of the unit.

Other features

At the back of the book you will find these four useful sections:

1 Answer key
2 Extended learning through COBUILD

In order to help you extend your vocabulary as you work through the material, further uses of key language are explored through references to examples taken from the Collins COBUILD Corpus. If you turn to page 101, you will find more information on meaning, usage, and collocations related to words used in the units.

3 How should I read? Choosing a reading approach
4 Improving your reading speed

We recommend you read *How should I read? Choosing a reading approach* and *Improving your reading speed* before you start using the course. These two sections have lots of useful tips.

Using *Reading*

You can either work through the units from Unit 1 to Unit 20, or you can pick and choose the units that are most useful to you. For example, you might want to concentrate on *Doing business* but spend less time on *Business media and books*. The Contents page will help you in your selection of units and your own plan for learning.

Keep a vocabulary notebook and, after completing each unit, add any new words from the text to your book.

Language level

Reading has been written to help business learners at B2 level and above (Upper Intermediate to Advanced).

Other titles

Also available in the *Collins English for Business* series: *Speaking, Listening*, and *Writing*.

1

Managing your inbox

Getting started

1 Scan over the new emails in Alex's inbox below and answer these questions.

1 Whose email should he read first and why?

....

2 Whose email has an attachment and what is it?

....

3 Whose email refers to plans for a future event and what is it?

....

From	Subject	Date received		
✉ Li Sung	Programme for conference	6 March 09.52	!!	
✉ Nora Stephens	Approval needed urgently	6 March 09.27		
✉ Ella Wood	James project update	6 March 09.23		
✉ Pierre Valois	Sales reports attached	6 March 09.15		📎
✉ Rose Mills	Interview confirmation	6 March 09.13		

2 Skim over the three emails opposite in just one minute. Which of the three emails might Alex leave until later to read in detail? Why?

....

1 | Dear all,

Please find below details for the company conference to be held on 23 April.

Conference venue: The Great Hall, Grants Hotel, London, W6 4AJ

Attendees: All senior management

Timetable for the day:

09.30	Welcome breakfast
10.00	Address from CEO
10.30	Annual financial results and budget for next year
11.30	Sales and Marketing annual review
12.30	HR presentation
13.30	Lunch
14.30	Strategic plan for next year: 'Greater and better'
16.30	Address from Managing Director
17.00	End

A detailed breakdown of all the day's presentations will be sent out in due course.

I apologize for the delay in circulating these details and if any changes are made, I'll be sure to keep you all in the loop.

Best wishes,

[................................]

Events Organizer

2 | Hi Alex,

Sorry for not getting back to you sooner with the information that you need for the conference – the sales reports that you asked for are attached.

Could you possibly take a look at January's figures because there are some loose ends that we need to tie up.

Look forward to hearing from you.

Thanks,

[................................]

Sales and Marketing Account Manager

3 | Dear Alex,
Please note that the deadline for budget approval was close of play yesterday.

I would appreciate it if you could give me the green light as soon as possible because I need to submit them to the board today.

Should you need any further information, please do not hesitate to contact me – I'm on extension 231.

I look forward to your reply.

Thank you in advance,

[................................]

Finance Manager

Understanding

 1 Insert the senders' names in the spaces in the three emails on the previous page.

2 Are the following statements True or False? Correct any that are false.

1 All employees are expected to attend the conference.

....

2 There may be further changes to the plans for the conference.

....

3 Pierre sent the sales reports to Alex as soon as he was asked.

....

4 There are some unresolved issues regarding July's figures.

....

5 Alex must approve the sales reports by 2 p.m. today.

....

6 Nora Stephens is planning to submit the budgets to the board by the end of today.

....

Developing your reading skills

1 What is the purpose of each of the emails? Tick the box(es) as appropriate.

	Email 1	Email 2	Email 3
To send Alex information about something	✓	✓	
To ask Alex to do something		✓	✓
To apologize about a delay in something		✓	
To invite a response from Alex regarding something		✓	✓

2 After reading his emails, Alex marks each with a note to prioritize his tasks. Match the comments to the emails that they refer to.

1 Email 1   **A** Approve budgets right away.

2 Email 2   **B** Not urgent, look at when time allows.

3 Email 3   **C** Look at first thing tomorrow to sort out unresolved issue.

Language focus

1 Fill the blanks in the sentences with one of the words or phrases from the box.

> attachment   bcc   cc   recipient   reply   reply all   sender   subject

1 The .... is the person who writes and sends an email and the ....
is the person who receives it.

2 The .... field or box is where you write a brief summary of the email contents.

3 An .... is a file that is sent along with an email.

4 .... is used in an email to indicate that a copy is being sent to another person, while .... is a way of sending an email to a number of recipients without revealing their email addresses to each other.

5 If you want to send an email back just to the sender, then you press ...., but if you want to send an email back to the sender and also to each person who received the original email, you press ....

2 Insert the expressions from the emails into the correct section of the box.

Should you need any further information, please do not hesitate to contact me.

Hi Alex,

Could you possibly ...?

~~Dear Alex,~~

I apologize for ...

I would appreciate it if you could ...

Look forward to hearing from you.

Please find below ...

Thanks,

Sorry for ...

Thank you in advance,

The sales reports are attached.

I look forward to your reply.

Purpose	More formal expression	Less formal expression
To start an email	*Dear Alex,*	
To advise about information sent with an email		
To ask somebody to do something		
To apologize about something		
To invite a response from the recipient		
To end an email/express gratitude		

3 Look at the idioms from the emails and write them with the correct definitions.

~~close of play~~ give somebody the green light on something   in due course   in the loop   some loose ends to tie up

1 end of the working day:
   close of play ....

2 fully informed about something:
   ....

3 some problems that still need to be solved:
   ....

4 when the time is right:
   ....

5 give permission for somebody to do something:
   ....

Review

How many emails do you receive each day? How do you manage your inbox? Remember to deal with the ones that are marked urgent and skim through emails that are not urgent, and come back to them when you have more time.

2 Dealing with group emails

Getting started

Skim through the series of five emails, which are presented with the most recent one first, in just 60 seconds and choose the best summary of the situation.

1 There has been a problem with the Traverse software, which manages the company's travel arrangements, that is resolved.

2 There is a problem with the Traverse software, which manages the company's travel arrangements, that is unresolved although they know how to solve the problem.

3 There is a problem with the Traverse software, which manages the company's travel arrangements, that is unresolved.

---

1 | Re: Meeting invitation

Sent: 4 April   11.36

To: Tom Becaveric; Xavier Justino; Jacky Miller; Ben Wade

Location: Meeting room 5
Date: 5 April
Time: 9.30 a.m.

To discuss: Double payment of commission to six external travel agencies

Please RSVP.

Regards,
Dina
PA to Finance Director
Blomfield Wright Travel Associates

---

2 | From: Tom Becarevic
Re: Overpayment of commission
Sent: 4 April   11.12

To: Ben Wade; Jacky Miller
Cc: Xavier Justino; Dina Finn

This is a serious issue.

Ben – please email the agencies immediately to inform them of the technical error. We'll advise about how we will resolve the matter in due course.

Xavier – we've had these problems with Traverse in the past. I thought they'd all been resolved by your team in IT. Please advise ASAP.

Dina – please arrange a meeting first thing tomorrow with Xavier, Jacky, and Ben so that we can get to the bottom of how this happened, figure out how to resolve it, and ensure it never happens again.

BW,
Tom
Finance Director
Blomfield Wright Travel Associates

---

3 | From: Ben Wade
Re: Overpayment of commission
Sent: 4 April   10.59
To: Jacky Miller; Tom Becaveric

Dear Both,
FYI, it looks like we've paid six agencies double their usual rate of commission this month, which equates to an overpayment of $150,000.

Best regards,
Ben
Sales team manager
Blomfield Wright Travel Associates

---

4 | From: Jacky Miller
Re: Overpayment of commission
Sent: 4 April   10.47
To: Ben Wade
Cc: Tom Becaveric

Dear Ben,
We need to get an idea of the scale of the problem as soon as possible. Please could you investigate exactly how much we're talking about here.

Tom – we had similar problems last year, which were supposed to have been resolved with the Traverse systems upgrade. Any thoughts?

Best,
Jacky
Sales Director
Blomfield Wright Travel Associates

---

5 | From: Ben Wade
Re: Overpayment of commission
Sent: 4 April   10.36
To: Jacky Miller

Dear Jacky,
It has come to my attention that we have paid double commission to some of our external travel agencies this month. This appears to have been caused by a glitch in the Traverse computer system. What are your thoughts on this?

Regards,
Ben
Sales team manager
Blomfield Wright Travel Associates

Understanding

Look again at the emails and answer these questions.

1 Why does Ben email Jacky in email 5?

....

2 Has this problem occurred before?

....

3 Who does Jacky bring into discussions and why?

....

4 How much money is involved?

....

5 Which two people does Tom bring into discussions and why?

....

6 What is happening tomorrow in an effort to resolve the issue?

....

Developing your reading skills

1 **Imagine that you are the Xavier, the IT Manager and you come to the group email late. Choose the best response.**

 1 I'm afraid that this is the first I've heard about this problem, but I'll get my team onto it straight away and update you at the meeting tomorrow.

 2 I'm afraid that this is the first I've heard about this problem, but I don't really want to get involved.

 3 I'm afraid that this is the first I've heard about this problem, but I'll email the external travel agencies to find out what went wrong.

2 **When you are copied into a long group email, you often need to scan through to find the exact details about a task that has been allocated to you. Match the person with the action point or action points.**

1	Xavier	..*B*...	4	Jacky	....
2	Ben	.... /........	5	Xavier, Tom, Ben, and Jacky	....
3	Dina	....			

A Set up a meeting for tomorrow morning and send out an email to invite the attendees.

B Find out exactly what went wrong with the Traverse system in time for tomorrow's meeting so that I can explain it to my colleagues.

C Prepare for and attend the meeting tomorrow at 9.30 a.m.

D Get Ben to find out exactly how much money we have overpaid.

E Find out how many agencies we've overpaid and let everybody concerned know the exact cost.

F Email the affected travel agencies to inform them of the technical error.

3   Sometimes you need to be able to 'read between the lines' to understand what people really feel and think about a difficult situation, that is to interpret what they really mean. Identify the speakers below by reading between the lines of their emails above.

~~Tom Becaveric~~   Xavier Justino   Jacky Miller   Ben Wade

1   I'm annoyed. I'm the one who's going to have to explain a $150,000 hole in this month's takings. How was this allowed to happen? I need some answers.
Tom Becaveric..

2   I'm worried. It sounds as though this was due to problems with the Traverse system, which I or my team should have spotted and resolved before it went live.

....

3   I'm frustrated. My team and I have had these problems with Traverse before and they should have been sorted out before any more mistakes were made.

....

4   I've discovered a problem and think I need to bring it to the attention of my superiors so that I don't get blamed for it.

....

Language focus

1   Group the phrases under the correct heading in the box.

~~Any thoughts?~~   Ben will circulate exact figures shortly.
I'll get back to you as soon as I can.   We will keep you updated.
Please advise ASAP.   What are your thoughts on this?

Phrases requesting further information	Phrases promising further information
Any thoughts?	

2   Complete the sentences with these words.

attention   bottom   get   present   glitch

1   She understands how urgent the situation is, so she's going to .... her team onto it right away.
2   It's not working – there must be a .... in the system.
3   Let's try to get to the .... of this issue, so that we can understand why it happened.
4   It has come to my .... that employees are using the Internet for non-work purposes.
5   I'm afraid I don't have all the information in front of me, so I can't comment at ....

Review

A colleague stops you in the corridor and says 'I hear the Traverse system is causing problems. Do you know what is happening?' Briefly explain the situation to your colleague from your reading of the emails.

3 Dealing with long emails

How to read long emails

Long emails require more time and attention than the short ones featured in Units 1 and 2.

- When you find a long email in your inbox, read the title and first paragraph carefully, then skim through the rest of it quickly to understand the gist and to make sure that it does not need an immediate reply. Then flag it to come back to once you have dealt with any short emails, which will not take up as much of your time.
- When you come back to the long email, determine what sort of reply is required, then either forward it to a colleague for him or her to deal with, or read it intensively so that you can take any action yourself.

Getting started

Read the title and first paragraph of Li Sung's email carefully, and skim over the rest in just 60 seconds. Then complete the sentence with the best option.

Li Sung is writing to Nicola Mann ...

1   ... to inform her of the excellent experience that her company had at the company conference held at Grants Hotel on 23 April.
2   ... to make plans for the upcoming conference at Grants Hotel on 23 April.
3   ... to complain about a number of factors regarding her company's conference held at Grants Hotel on 23 April.

From: Li Sung

Re: Various issues regarding conference 23 April

Date: 3 May   9.37

To: Nicola Mann

Dear Nicola Mann,

On 23 April, we hired The Great Hall at Grants Hotel for our company conference. Unfortunately there were a number of factors that were unsatisfactory.

Firstly, the equipment supplied was defective. I had informed your Conference Planner, Jason Philips, that we would require access to projectors for presenting material from laptop computers during the presentations. In the event, he was unable to locate a projector and we had to get one sent from our offices at our own expense.

Secondly, the facilities were disappointing. The conference room was overheated and materials from the previous day's conference were left lying around. When I arrived in the morning, there were not enough tables and chairs supplied, which meant the day's proceedings were delayed while extras were found and set up.

Finally, the catering was poor and not what we would expect of a four star hotel. I am afraid that the service was delayed and, when the food finally reached us, it was lukewarm and fairly mediocre.

I look forward to receiving a response.

Best wishes,
Li Sung
Events Organiser

Understanding

1 You are Nicola Mann. Underline the key sentences that highlight Li Sung's complaints, and make notes so that you can address each point in turn in your response.

Now read Nicola Mann's reply to Li Sung.

From: Nicola Mann
Re: Various issues regarding conference 23 April
Date: 5 May   15.46
To: Li Sung

Dear Li Sung,

I am writing in response to your email of 3 May.

Firstly, please accept our sincere apologies for the incidents that occurred during your conference at Grants Hotel in April. Customer satisfaction is of paramount importance to us, and I regret that, on this occasion, we fell short of your requirements.

To address each of the points that you raise in turn:

- I spoke to Jason Philips about the equipment problems and the hotel does have three projectors. Regretfully, all were out of order on 23 April due to circumstances beyond our control. Please rest assured that this was an isolated incident, which we'll ensure never reoccurs. As a leading international conference centre, we pride ourselves on our state-of-the art equipment.

- With regards to the state of the facilities, the problem arose because of an error in our internal checks. Having said this, there is really no excuse for it and I apologize for this. I have asked Housekeeping to implement a new system of checking conference rooms prior to events to ensure that such problems do not reoccur.

- I discussed the issues that you raised about your lunch with our Food and Beverages Manager, and unfortunately the problems that day resulted from an unusually high number of kitchen staff being off sick. We have since changed our staffing rota to ensure that we always have sufficient cover available should such a situation happen again. I'll personally ensure that this never happens again.

As a gesture of goodwill, I propose that we reimburse you the cost of transporting your own projector to the hotel. Additionally, we can offer you a 10 per cent discount on your next conference booking with us.

In conclusion, I hope that this meets with your approval and we look forward to welcoming you again soon at Grants Hotel, London.

Do not hesitate to contact me if there is any way that I can assist further.

Sincerely,
Nicola Mann
Manager, Grants Hotel

2 You are now Li Sung. Make notes on the following points to feed back to your supervisor.

1 What were the reasons that Nicola Mann gave to explain each complaint?

   1 *Equipment: The hotel has three projectors but all were out of order due to circumstances beyond their control.* ....

   2 ....

   3 ....

2 What compensation/resolution for the future did she offer for each issue?

   1 ....

   2 ....

   3 ....

Developing your reading skills

1 In her response to Li Sung's complaint, Nicola Mann notes that she has taken action on each of the issues raised. What do you think she might have said in her emails to the following employees?

1 Jason Philips, Conference Planner

I've had a complaint from Li Sung regarding the fact that we didn't have any projectors available for her conference. Please advise ASAP on how this was allowed to happen. ....

2 Jan Harding, Housekeeping Manager

....

....

3 Helen Taylor, Head of Catering

....

....

2 Read between the lines of these quotations from the emails and choose the option that best expresses what the writer <u>really</u> means in each case.

1 I had informed your Conference Planner, Jason Philips, that we would require access to projectors ... In the event, he was unable to locate a projector.

   A It wasn't Jason Philips' fault that we didn't have a projector.

   B It was Jason Philips' fault that we didn't have a projector. ✓

   C We should have told Jason Philips that we wanted a projector.

2 I look forward to receiving a response.

   A I don't expect a reply to this email.

   B I expect a reply to this email soon.

   C You can reply if you like.

3 due to circumstances beyond our control

   A It wasn't our fault.

   B It was our fault.

   C It was your fault.

4 The problem arose because of an error in our internal checks.

   A We checked the room properly.

   B We didn't check the room properly.

   C Somebody else checked the room.

5 As a gesture of goodwill, ...

   A I'm about to offer you some form of compensation, even though we're not legally obliged to ...

   B We won't be offering you anything ...

   C We are legally obliged to give you a refund ...

Language focus

When reading long emails, you may have to deal with more formal language. Look again at the expressions that Nicola Mann uses in her email to deal with a complaint. Insert the headings below into A, B, C and D to show the purpose of each set of expressions.

1 ~~To explain the reasons for the problems~~

2 To offer compensation

3 To apologize

4 To provide reassurance that the problems will not happen again

A	B *To explain the reasons for the problems*
Please accept our sincere apologies for ... I regret that we fell short of your requirements. There is really no excuse for it and I apologize for this.	The problem arose because of ... Unfortunately the problems that day resulted from ... ... due to circumstances beyond our control.
C	**D**
... to ensure that such problems do not reoccur. I'll personally ensure that this never happens again. Please rest assured that this was an isolated incident, which we'll ensure never reoccurs.	As a gesture of goodwill, I propose that we ... Additionally, we can offer ...

Review

You are Li Sung and your supervisor has asked for an update. Brief her on how Nicola Mann responded to your complaint.

4 Understanding organizations

How to read materials related to company organization

Companies present who they are and what they do in a range of ways, through business cards, company organization charts and biographies of key employees.

- Scan over business cards to find out somebody's contact information or profession.
- Skim over company organization charts to get a general idea of the company structure, for example whether it has a flat or a hierarchical structure.
- Study company organization charts carefully to find out who you need to speak to in particular situations or to understand the reporting lines within a particular department.

Getting started

Scan over the business cards in 30 seconds and match the people to their industries. Then learn about Ayisha Khabbazeh from the organizational chart and biography.

1	Ayisha Khabbazeh	A	Interior design
2	Nicola Mann	B	Manufacturing
3	Charlotte Ring	C	Hotel management
4	Peter Harrop	D	Photography

1

Ayisha Khabbazeh | President and CEO

FORDHAMS & CO. MANUFACTURING

www.fordhamsandcomanufacturing.com

Chariot House
67-69 Blackfield Way
London WC6 4HS, UK
+44 207 362 8987

Pan Yu Street
Shanghai 200035
China
+86 21 3829 2922

2

Nicola Mann
Manager
nmann@grants.co.uk
www.grantshotel.com
T: 207 2839 2839

Grants
HOTEL

LIBERTY WAY, LONDON, W6 4AJ

3

398 36th Street • New York • NY • 20018 • USA

RINGS DESIGN SERVICES

CHARLOTTE RING • INTERIOR DESIGNER

No job too small, no job too big. Trust in me to transform your space.

Tel: +1 212 239 2928
Email: ringsdesignservices@contact.com
Follow me on Twitter: Charlotte_The_Designer
Find me on LinkedIn: Charlotte H Ring

4

PETER HARROP
PH
PHOTOGRAPHER

www.peterharrop.com

Fordhams and Co. – Company Organization Chart

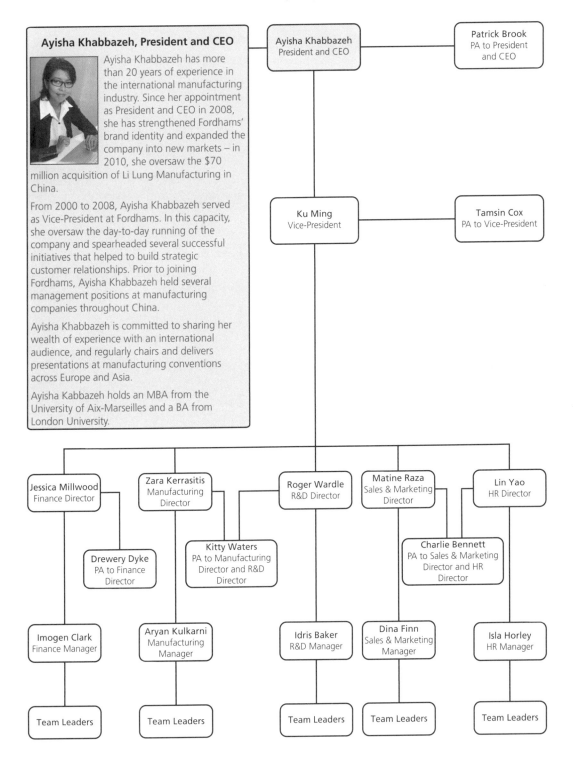

Ayisha Khabbazeh, President and CEO

Ayisha Khabbazeh has more than 20 years of experience in the international manufacturing industry. Since her appointment as President and CEO in 2008, she has strengthened Fordhams' brand identity and expanded the company into new markets – in 2010, she oversaw the $70 million acquisition of Li Lung Manufacturing in China.

From 2000 to 2008, Ayisha Khabbazeh served as Vice-President at Fordhams. In this capacity, she oversaw the day-to-day running of the company and spearheaded several successful initiatives that helped to build strategic customer relationships. Prior to joining Fordhams, Ayisha Khabbazeh held several management positions at manufacturing companies throughout China.

Ayisha Khabbazeh is committed to sharing her wealth of experience with an international audience, and regularly chairs and delivers presentations at manufacturing conventions across Europe and Asia.

Ayisha Kabbazeh holds an MBA from the University of Aix-Marseilles and a BA from London University.

Ayisha Khabbazeh — President and CEO

Patrick Brook — PA to President and CEO

Ku Ming — Vice-President

Tamsin Cox — PA to Vice-President

Jessica Millwood — Finance Director

Zara Kerrasitis — Manufacturing Director

Roger Wardle — R&D Director

Matine Raza — Sales & Marketing Director

Lin Yao — HR Director

Drewery Dyke — PA to Finance Director

Kitty Waters — PA to Manufacturing Director and R&D Director

Charlie Bennett — PA to Sales & Marketing Director and HR Director

Imogen Clark — Finance Manager

Aryan Kulkarni — Manufacturing Manager

Idris Baker — R&D Manager

Dina Finn — Sales & Marketing Manager

Isla Horley — HR Manager

Team Leaders

Team Leaders

Team Leaders

Team Leaders

Team Leaders

Understanding

Are the following statements True or False? Correct any that are false.

Business cards:

1   Charlotte Ring works for a company that has offices in Shanghai and London.

....

2   Nicola Mann is the manager of Grants Hotel.

....

Company organization chart:

3   Patrick Brook is PA to Ku Ming.

....

4   The directors of Fordhams and Co. all have their own individual PAs.

....

Biography:

5   Ayisha Khabbazeh has been at Fordhams since 2008.

....

6   As President and CEO, she oversees the daily operations of the company and develops strategic customer relationships.

....

Developing your reading skills

1   Scan over the business cards to answer the following queries from colleagues.

1   'Do you know Peter Harrop's telephone number?'
No, but I've got his website address, so you could try that – www.peterharrop.com.

2   'Do you have Charlotte Ring's email address?'

....

3   'Do you know if Fordhams and Co. has more than one office?'

....

4   'Do you have the name and number of the manager of Grants Hotel?'

....

2   Use the company organization chart to help you work out the person you should speak to in the following situations.

1   To arrange a time to see the R&D Director
Kitty Waters, PA to R&D Director

2   To ask somebody to write and submit a job advertisement

....

3   To answer a query about next year's budgets

....

4   To discuss a very serious problem that must be addressed by the most senior person in the company

....

5   To discuss an idea that you've had for an online promotional campaign

....

6   To invite Ku Ming to a meeting

....

Language focus

1   When reading company organization charts, you need to be able to describe the relationships between people within an organization. Write the words in bold in the correct column in the box below.

Imogen Clark ~~is a direct report of~~ the Finance Director.

The Finance Director **is managed by** the Vice-President.

The R&D Director **collaborates with** the Manufacturing Director.

Dina Finn **manages** a team of six Team Leaders.

Craig Portland **oversees** the Finance Team Leaders.

The Vice-President **reports to/into** the CEO.

Lin Yao **supervises** the HR Manager.

Jessica Millwood **works with** Zara Kerrasitis.

Work in a more senior position to somebody	Work at the same level as somebody	Work for somebody
		be a direct report of

2   Look again at the organizational chart on page 17 and insert one of the expressions from the box in Language Focus 1 to make these sentences correct. Do not use the same expression more than once.

1   Ayisha Khabbazeh ....*oversees*........ Fordhams and Co.
2   Zara Kerrasitis .... Roger Wardle.
3   Jessica Millwood .... Ku Ming.
4   Jessica Millwood .... Imogen Clark.
5   Kitty Waters .... Zara Kerrasitis and Roger Wardle.
6   Matine Raza .... Lin Yao.
7   Isla Horley .... the HR Team Leaders.
8   Aryan Kulkarni .... Zara Kerrasitis.
9   Idris Baker .... Dina Finn.

Review

You meet up with a former colleague who wants to know all about your current position. Answer their questions: 'What's your job title?', 'Who/what team(s) do you work with?', 'Who do you report into?'

5 Managing schedules and budgets

How to read schedules and budgets

A schedule is a plan that gives a list of events or tasks and the times by which each one should be completed. A budget is a plan showing how much money a business has available to spend on the various parts of a project. It may also include a forecast to show how much profit the business hopes to make based on the revenue generated compared to the costs.

- Skim through a schedule to get the gist of the main stages of the process.
- Scan over a budget to get a general idea of how much is to be spent in each area.
- When you find a section of a schedule or budget that you are responsible for, take as much time as you need to read intensively for detail, making sure that you understand every word, and using a dictionary if necessary.

Getting started

Bellhill Construction plc has just won the bidding process to build Hill View School. Below is the draft budget and on the page opposite is the schedule for phase one of the project.

You are the Commercial Director, in charge of the commercial team. Skim over the schedule and highlight the sections that you and your team are directly involved with. Write down the key dates.

PROJECT BUDGET

Project Director	J Olympios	Project		Hill View School
		$m		
CONTRACT VALUE		32.8	A	
COSTS:				
Design consultants & architectural		0.9		
Legal fees		0.6		
Demolition and site clearance		0.4		
Structural works		6.2		
Mechanical & engineering works		5.8		
Subcontractor cost		5.6		
Equipment hire and materials		3.0		
Labour hire		0.9		
Management & site team		1.2		
Central overhead costs		3.6		
Cost contingency		1.6		
TOTAL COSTS		29.8	B	
FORECAST PROFIT (A-B)		3.0		
FORECAST PROFIT PERCENTAGE		9.1%		

Bellhill Construction plc

PROJECT SCHEDULE: PHASE ONE: DESIGN FINALIZATION AND CONTRACTUAL COMPLETION

Project	Hill View School
Project Director	J Olympios

Design

TASK	DUE DATE	RESPONSIBILITY
Meeting with client to discuss amendments to draft one designs	17 April	Design team, commercial team and client
Revised designs submitted to commercial team	30 April	Design team
Cost assessment of design revisions submitted to Commercial Director and CEO	7 May	Commercial team
In-house approval of new costings and design revisions	31 May	Commercial Director, CEO and Board of Governors
Final designs submitted to client	1 June	Design team
Final designs approved by client	15 June	Client

Legal and contractual work

TASK	DUE DATE	RESPONSIBILITY
Delivery of draft contract to client	20 April	Legal team
Site survey commissioned	3 May	External surveyors and legal team
Planning applications submitted	5 May	Legal team
Feedback on draft contract from client	14 May	Client
Site survey completed	17 May	External surveyors and legal team
Public consultation meeting	18 May	PR team
Revised contract sent to client	20 May	Legal team
All contractual details finalized	31 May	Legal team and client
Planning application approved	5 June	Legal team
Final contracts signed	15 June	CEO and client

Understanding

Answer these questions about the schedule and budget.

1 By what date must the commercial team submit their cost assessment of the design revisions to the Commercial Director and CEO?

....

2 By what date must the client and the legal team have the contracts finalized?

....

3 What's the final deadline for signing contracts and approving the final designs?

....

4 How much money in the budget has been allocated to paying lawyers' fees?

....

5 How much contingency has been allowed in the budget?

....

6 What's the forecasted profit for this project?

....

Developing your reading skills

1 You are the main client co-ordinator on the project. Pick out the key stages that the client will need to be involved in and complete the email.

To: KayAnderson@citycouncil.com

From: j.marino@bellhillconstructionplc.com

Re: Hill View School building

Dear Ms Anderson,

My name is James Marino and I am your main point of contact at Bellhill Construction plc.

I've received a schedule for the key dates over the next three months. Please be advised of the following dates where we will require your input.

17 April *Meeting with our design and commercial team to discuss amendments to the draft designs.*

20 April ....

14 May ....

20 May ....

31 May ....

1 June ....

15 June ....

....

Do let me know if any of these dates will be difficult for you or if you have any queries. I very much look forward to working with you over the coming months.

Best wishes,

James Marino

---

2 The budget was put together based on a previous project of similar size. However, you have just received the following email, relating to some late costs that were added onto that project. Read the email, fill the blanks in the box below to update the budget for Hill View, and finally answer the question that follows.

Dear James,

As discussed we had some cost overruns on the Meridian Way School, which could impact on your budget for Hill View. The additional costs were:

Design and architectural $0.3 million
Site clearance $0.1 million
Mechanical/engineering $0.7 million
Labour hire $0.1 million

With the benefit of hindsight, these were all costs that should have been foreseen in our original budget on Meridian Way. Give me a call if you would like to discuss.

Best,
Graham

Budget area	Hill View original budget	Meridian Way additional costs	Updated Hill View budget
1 Design and architectural	$0.9 million	$0.3 million	$1.2 million
2 Site clearance	0.6	0.1	0.7
3 Mechanical/engineering	5.0		6.0
4 Labour hire	0.4		

What's the new forecast profit after making these budget revisions?

....

Language focus

Match the verbs with their meanings.

1 submit
2 commission
3 approve
4 sign
5 complete
6 finalize
7 revise

A prepare a new edited version of something
B formally give your consent to something
C make something final
D finish something
E send something to somebody for consideration
F allocate a task to somebody
G write your signature

Review

Kay Anderson approved all the schedule dates that you emailed her in 'Developing your reading skills 1'. Now write an email to your boss detailing any changes that might need to be made to the schedule or budget. Remember to refer back to 'Developing your reading skills 2'.

Reading agendas and minutes

How to read agendas and minutes

An agenda is distributed before a meeting to tell you the points for discussion. The minutes of a meeting are circulated after a meeting to provide a written record of what was discussed and agreed, and action points.

- Read agendas carefully so that you know exactly when and where a meeting is taking place, and so that you can prepare fully and anticipate any questions that you might be asked about the topics under discussion.

- Skim through the minutes of a meeting, reading any sections that are relevant to you in detail. Make sure that your words have been recorded accurately and that you are aware of any tasks that have been allocated to you. You will have to approve the minutes at the next meeting.

Getting started

Read the agenda below and tick what preparation you would need to do for this meeting. Then read the minutes of this meeting.

1 Read the minutes from the last meeting, so that I will be in a position to approve them. ✓

2 Remind myself about the company's health and safety policies.

✓ 3 Read the March sales report.

4 Read the July sales report.

5 Revise my sales targets.

✓ 6 Think about any points to raise during AOB.

SALES & MARKETING MONTHLY MEETING

Date: 3 April   *Time:* 10.30   *Venue:* Meeting room 6

Called by: Sara Filfil (Sales & Marketing Director and Chair)

Attendees: All Sales Representatives: Hannah Pepper, Jack Stone, Adam Lamb, Tanya Prakash, Khem Singh.

Recording secretary: Rory Morgan.

Please read: March sales report attached.   *Please bring:* n/a

AGENDA

1	Apologies	4 Sales results for March
2	Approval of minutes of last meeting	5 New incentives and rewards
3	Matters arising	6 AOB (any other business)

MINUTES OF SALES & MARKETING MONTHLY MEETING

The monthly Sales & Marketing meeting of Philips Pharmaceutical Sales was held at 10.30 on 3 April at offices of company.

Attendees

Sara Filfil (Chair), Hannah Pepper, Adam Lamb, Tanya Prakash, Khem Singh, Rory Morgan

Apologies

Jack Stone sent apologies because unwell.

Approval of Minutes

Rory Morgan presented minutes of Sales & Marketing Monthly meeting, 4 March for approval. Unanimously approved as presented.

Matters arising

- Adam Lamb noted that order not yet placed for new SJE12 sales software, approved at last meeting.
- Sara Filfil to purchase before next meeting.

Sales results for March

Sara Filfil drew attention to March sales report:

- Sara Filfil noted that sales were down by 2.4% on previous month.
- Adam Lamb suggested possible cause was special promotion run by Mastersons Pharmaceuticals. Adam Lamb to research upcoming promotions by major competitors for presentation at next meeting.
- Sara Filfil noted that despite drop in sales all employees met individual sales targets. Special commendation given to Hannah Pepper who exceeded target by 8%.

New incentives and rewards

Sara Filfil announced two new initiatives and rewards:

- If a Sales Representative exceeds sales targets by more than 15%, they will receive increased commission of 7.5% of total revenue on all subsequent sales.
- In December, a five-star holiday for a family of four will be awarded to Sales Representative with highest quantity of sales during year.

AOB

- Tanya Prakash to circulate sample version of new quarterly newsletter by 15 April.
- All attendees to provide feedback on newsletter to Tanya Prakash by end of month.
- Hannah Pepper to coordinate collection for HR Director's maternity present by 8 April.

Understanding

Answer these questions about the agenda and minutes of the meeting.

1   What time did the Sales & Marketing monthly meeting start and where was it held?

   ....

2   Who was the Chair of the meeting and who took minutes?

   ....

3   What action point from the last meeting did Adam Lamb draw attention to?

   ....

4   Are sales for March up or down on the previous month?

   ....

5   Who failed to meet their sales targets this month?

   ....

6   Which sales representative was singled out with a special commendation?

   ....

Developing your reading skills

1   Extract the action points and deadlines from the minutes to fill the blanks below.

Attendee	Action point	Deadline
Sara Filfil	To purchase SJE12 sales software	By next meeting
Adam Lamb		
Tanya Prakash		
All attendees		
Hannah Pepper		

2   It's important that the minutes of a meeting should accurately reflect what was said by the attendees. Were the following statements that were made in the meeting recorded accurately or inaccurately?

1   Adam Lamb said 'Can I just say that the new SJE12 sales software, which was approved at the last meeting, hasn't been ordered yet.'

   (Accurate)   Inaccurate

2   Sara Filfil said 'I'll get the order in for the new software before our next meeting.'

   Accurate   Inaccurate

3   Sara Filfil said 'Unfortunately, our sales results are down 3.6% on March's figure.'

   Accurate   Inaccurate

4   Adam Lamb said 'Yes, Mastersons Pharmaceuticals have been running a special promotion this month and it's hit us pretty hard.'

   Accurate   Inaccurate

5   Sara Filfil said 'Can I just make special reference to Hannah Pepper who sold the most this month, smashing her target by a massive 12%. Well done Hannah for doing so well in a difficult month!'

Accurate   Inaccurate

6   Khem Singh said 'I'll organize a collection for Sue before she goes off on maternity leave.'

Accurate   Inaccurate

Language focus

1   **Match these terms with their meanings.**

1 Venue/location
2 Called by
3 Chair
4 Attendee/ participant
5 Recording secretary
6 Apologies
7 Approval of minutes of last meeting
8 Matters arising/ action points
9 AOB
10 n/a

A   the person who controls the meeting, ensuring that it runs to time and that all points of the agenda are covered

B   a person who is present at the meeting

C   the place where the meeting takes place

D   short for 'Any Other Business': the point at which people can raise other issues that are not on the agenda

E   the person who takes notes during the meeting and will write up and distribute the minutes of the meeting

F   a message sent to a meeting to advise that one of the attendees will be unable to attend

G   short for 'not applicable': this explains a lack of information in a field or on a form because it is not relevant to the situation

H   arranged by someone for a particular time

I   the point in the meeting when those present at the last meeting must state that they are happy with the minutes from that meeting

J   issues for discussion

2   **Rewrite the action points, replacing the underlined verbs or phrases with one of the words or phrases from the box that has the same meaning.**

purchase	research	~~circulate~~	provide feedback on	coordinate

1   Kay Peterson to <u>send</u> annual report to all board members.
Kay Peterson to circulate annual report to all board members. ....

2   Nicky Chisholm to <u>investigate</u> ways of reducing overheads.
....

3   Roz Toole to <u>buy</u> new photocopier for department.
....

4   Sophie Jesman to <u>organize</u> a meeting with all department heads.
....

5   Liam Chu to <u>give comments about</u> presentations at company conference.
....

Review

Jack Stone is back at work the following day and asks you what the main points of the meeting were? Summarize the most important points discussed at the meeting.

7

Reading CVs and covering letters

How to read CVs and covering letters

A CV (curriculum vitae) or résumé, is a summary of a person's qualifications and work experience. This is usually sent in application for a job, together with a covering letter, which summarize the candidate's suitability for the job.

- Skim through a CV quickly to get the gist of whether a candidate is suitable for a particular position, and whether it is worth reading on in more detail.
- Scan over a CV to see if a candidate has the specific skills that you are looking for.

Getting started

1 You are recruiting a Financial Controller. Skim through this letter. Will you take the time to read this CV or will you discard it? Explain your answer.

....

2 Now skim through the CV on the next page. Do you think it's worth taking the time to read it in detail?

....

192 Kings Avenue
London E3 4AJ

Sophia Henry
Financial Director, Camen Engineering
23 Nialls Avenue
London WC2 4FA

8 March

Dear Ms Henry,

Re: Position of Financial Controller

I am writing in response to your job advertisement in the *Business Daily* newspaper on 4 March for a Financial Controller.

I am a fully qualified accountant with 12 years' post-qualification experience. In my current role as Senior Finance Manager at Desmarais UK, I am responsible for the day-to-day financial activities of the company and manage a team of 12 accountants. I have had extensive experience of working under pressure and keeping to tight deadlines. Similarly, I have a proven track record when it comes to multi-tasking.

The reason that I am looking for a new position is that my company has recently relocated to Kent and I am looking to find a job closer to home.

I enclose my CV and look forward to hearing from you in due course.

Yours sincerely,

Stephen Nicholas

STEPHEN NICHOLAS – CV

Mobile: 07722 382 228   **Email:** smonicholas@onlineworld.com

WORK EXPERIENCE

Nov 05 – Present	**Desmarais Construction UK Ltd**, Kent, UK
	(Construction, turnover for this year £280m. Subsidiary of Desmarais Group, turnover for this year 7.4b)
	Senior Finance Manager, leading team of 12 staff responsible for all financial reporting to Group under IFRS, local reporting under UK GAAP, purchase/sales ledgers, local/expatriate payroll, and all aspects of tax and treasury management. Promoted in July 2007 and January 2009.
	• Overhauled all financial and treasury reporting, significantly improving efficiency, accuracy and presentation.
	• Directly responsible for managing all external audits (three per year).
Jun 02 – Oct 05	**The Charalambous Group**, Cyprus
	(Financial services group providing company formation, accounting and tax planning services)
	Financial Controller, leading a team of four staff with responsibility for all client-based and in-house accounting and taxation.
	• Co-ordinated the production of accounts and financial statements for portfolio of over 200 client companies.
	• Prepared and submitted corporation tax and VAT returns, and dealt with any tax enquiries from UK/Cypriot tax authorities.
	• Liaised with clients on all aspects of accounting and taxation.
Sep 98 – May 02	**Burnett, Philips and Price**, London, UK
	(Global financial services)
	Assistant Manager in the Financial & Capital Markets Division, responsible for the audit of investment banks, stockbrokers, fund managers and some non-financial clients.

QUALIFICATIONS

Professional:	Qualified accountant (qualified in 2001, all exams passed first time)
University:	London University (UCL) BA Honours degree in Geography (2:1)
Education:	Southgate School, Ipswich 3 A levels, 1 AS level, 9 GCSEs

COMPETENCIES AND INTERESTS

IT skills:	MS Office (very strong Excel skills), SAP, JDE Edwards One World, Horizons Access Accounts.
Interests:	Running, swimming, reading.
REFEREES	Available on request

Understanding

Are the following statements True or False? Correct any that are false.

1 Stephen Nicholas is a part-qualified accountant with 12 years' post-qualification experience.

....

2 He currently works for Desmarais Construction UK Ltd.

....

3 He is looking for a new job because he is ambitious and there is no room for progression in his current company.

....

4 He has had experience in the food industry.

....

5 He has been promoted twice at his current company.

....

6 He has never worked outside the UK.

....

Developing your reading skills

1 **Analyse the structure of the covering letter and put the sections into the correct order.**

☐ A A concluding paragraph to draw attention to the CV that is enclosed with your letter (or attached with your email).

☐ B A paragraph to show how your experience and personal skills tie in with the job requirements.

☐ 1 C A reference line to summarize for the recipient what your letter is about.

☐ D An explanation of why you are looking for a new position.

☐ E An introductory paragraph explaining what position you are applying for and where you saw it advertised.

2 **Below are the key requirements for the position. Compare them to Stephen's CV, and tick those that he claims to fulfil.**

Experience/qualifications required
- qualified accountant + five years of experience ✓
- experience of managing a team

Competencies required
- knowledge of UKGAAP and IFRS
- excellent Excel skills

Qualities required
- ability to multi-task
- attention to detail
- ability to work under pressure to tight deadlines
- good communication skills

Language focus

1 Place the words from the CV into the correct place in the box.

~~qualifications~~   referee

interests   skill

competency   responsibility

work experience

Definition	CV word/phrase
a term to describe your employment history to date	
a person who knows you well and is prepared to write a letter on your behalf about your character and abilities	referee
the knowledge and ability to do something well	skill
examinations that you have passed	qualifications
the things that you enjoy doing	interest
the ability to carry out a job or task	
something that you are required to do as part of your job	

2 Match the verbs from the CV with their meanings.

1 **overhauled** all financial and treasury reporting ...

2 **participated in** training programme ...

3 **coordinated** the production of accounts and financial statements ...

4 **submitted** corporation tax and VAT returns ...

5 **liaised with** clients ...

A communicated and stayed in contact with

B handed over formally

C made changes in order to improve

D organized

E took part in

3 Fill the blanks with the correct preposition.

1 I have extensive experience *of* managing a team.

2 I was responsible .... recruiting all new employees.

3 I have had extensive experience of working .... pressure.

4 I manage a team .... 12 accountants.

5 My company has relocated .... Paris.

Review

You and your colleague from HR are about to interview Stephen for the position. Your colleague, however, hasn't had time to read the CV in detail. Summarize the key points of Stephen's CV in two sentences, and explain if you think he is a good candidate and why.

8

Studying job descriptions

How to read job descriptions

You will read job descriptions when applying for a new job or recruiting new employees. As an employee or manager, you also need to refer to job descriptions regularly as part of performance reviews.

- When looking for a job, read job descriptions intensively for detail to find out exactly what the recruiter is looking for and whether you are a good match for the position.
- When recruiting for a particular position, read the job description intensively for detail to make sure that you find a candidate who matches all the criteria.
- When reading a job description as part of a performance review, read the responsibilities and outcomes intensively and compare them with the achievements of the employee over the period.

Getting started

Scan over the job description in just 30 seconds and choose the best description of the job described.

1. A Financial Director at a leading engineering company.
2. A Financial Controller at a leading engineering company.
3. A Financial Controller at a leading accountancy firm.

<u>Job title</u>	Financial Controller
<u>The company</u>	

A leading engineering company that manufactures bespoke engineering components for distribution worldwide.

<u>Department/division</u>	Finance
<u>Reports to</u>	Financial Director
<u>The role</u>	

As Financial Controller, you will be responsible for the day-to-day financial activities of the company. This role would suit a fully qualified accountant with at least five years' post-qualification work experience.

Responsibility	Result/Outcomes
Financial management • Preparing monthly financial reporting pack for the Board of Directors. • Developing strategies to ensure effective management of company's finances.	• Directors are fully informed of monthly finances. • Finances are managed in the most cost-effective way both now and going forward.
Department management • Overseeing the internal accounting system to ensure effective management of accounts. • Managing a team of 12 accountants.	• Internal accounting systems function to maximum efficiency. • Finance department runs smoothly and in the most efficient way.
External accounting standards • Drafting statutory accounts for company that comply with all relevant accounting standards. • Liaising with external auditors and supplying them with all relevant information.	• Statutory accounts are produced in a timely and effective manner to the satisfaction of the Board and external accounting bodies. • Quarterly and annual audits run smoothly.

Person specification

Requirements	Essential	Desirable
Qualifications	Fully qualified accountant	• MBA
Experience	• Five years' post-qualification work experience • Proven track record of managing a team	• Previous experience within the engineering industry
Competencies	• Up-to-date knowledge of UKGAAP and International Financial Reporting Standards (IFRS) • Excellent Excel skills • Clear, effective communication skills • Good people management skills	• Good competency using other basic software packages, e.g. Word, Outlook
Disposition	• Full of energy and drive • Proactive self-starter • Able to multi-task while still paying attention to detail • Team player • Able to work well under pressure	• Able to think laterally

Understanding

Answer the following questions.

1 What does the company produce?

....

2 What is the Senior Financial Controller responsible for?

....

3 What qualifications does the Financial Controller need?

....

4 What sort of experience is essential for the position?

....

5 What sort of person does the candidate need to be?

....

Developing your reading skills

1 **Read the following extracts from covering letters, and tick the applicants whose experience matches the job description criteria.**

1 'I'm a fully qualified accountant with eight years' post-qualification experience.'
2 'I'm a part-qualified accountant with seven years' work experience in an accounts department.'
3 'I have five years' experience in sales within the engineering industry, but have never done accounts.'
4 'I have never worked in the engineering industry, but I have managed a team of accountants for seven years.'
5 'I'm a big-picture person rather than a detail person.'
6 'I'm used to working in stressful situations and actually work better in those conditions.'

2 **You are the Finance Director carrying out a performance review with the Financial Controller. Read the extracts from the appraisal form, match the achievements with the job requirements, and then give the employee a rating in each area.**

Rating system	1 Exceeding expectations
	2 Achieving expectations
	3 Not meeting expectations

Extract from appraisal form	Requirement as set out in job description	Rating
1 I have put in place a two-year plan to reduce operating costs by 10%.	• *Developing strategies to ensure effective management of company's finances.*	2
2 I have produced the financial pack on time every month and circulated it to all directors.		

Extract from appraisal form	Requirement as set out in job description	Rating
3 I have managed the Finance team of 12 effectively, and have successfully recruited two new employees.		
4 I have overseen the production of statutory accounts that were satisfactory both internally and externally.		
5 I worked with the auditors to answer queries relating to my department. Also, I dealt with questions relating to Accounts Receivable department because manager was on leave during the audit.		
6 There were some issues with the internal accounting system, which I should have addressed earlier. These have now been resolved and one of my objectives is to ensure that such problems do not reoccur.		

Language focus

Fill the blanks in the sentences with one of the words or phrases from the box to describe a person's competencies.

proactive self-starter
proven track record
multi-task
attention to detail

under pressure
communication skills
energy and drive
team player

1   He's very good at conveying information to other people – he has excellent ....
2   She's got a .... in sales – just look at the glowing reference she has from the Sales Director of her previous company.
3   She's a .... – she always gets the job done without having to be reminded.
4   He seems to very enthusiastic and ambitious – he's got lots of ....
5   I've seen her .... – sometimes she's juggling several things at one time.
6   He never seems to get stressed and in fact works better ....
7   She works very well with the other people in the department – she's a real ....
8   He's great at spotting even the tiniest of mistakes – he pays ....

Review

You decide to apply for the position. Write the covering letter that you will send with your CV, demonstrating how you have the skills and experience required to fulfil all the criteria for the job. Use the covering letter in Unit 7 as a model.

9 Analysing business reports

Getting started

Read the Contents page opposite. Which section of the report would you turn to in the following situations? Insert your answers into the table below. Then read the Executive summary.

In order to:	Report section
• read the main part of the report detailing the information that has been discovered	*Main findings*
• know why the report was commissioned	
• read a short summary of the 'Main Findings' section	
• focus on suggestions of how any issues or problems could be dealt with	
• read a summary of all the key points in each section of report	
• find out exactly what appears on each page of the report	
• know about methods that were used to carry out the research contained in the report	
• know if there is any additional relevant information which is not directly related to the subject of the report	

Contents

Executive summary

This report was commissioned by the Board of Governors of FlySky Airlines to investigate why passenger numbers on their transatlantic flights dropped by 4% over the period June to December 2011, and business bookings for premium seats were down by 18% over the same period. The report advises on how to improve ticket sales in the face of this downturn.

Methods of analysis included market research amongst previous customers and existing customers, an investigation into the workings of the main competitors in the transatlantic market, and an examination of general trends in passenger movements.

Results of data analysed show that FlySky Airlines' ticket sales dropped for the following reasons:

- the economic slowdown in North America and global recession has meant a general reduction in passenger numbers on all routes.
- the increase in video-conferencing has led to less business travel on all routes.
- cuts in company travel budgets have meant that business customers who previously booked premium seats now choose economy seats.
- intense competition from cut-price online airlines who undercut FlySky Airlines' ticket prices by as much as 20%.
- general dissatisfaction amongst business customers regarding increased check-in time requirements for passengers flying in premium seats.
- low morale amongst cabin crew following unresolved dispute surrounding working hours, which is having a knock-on effect on passengers.

The report concludes that, although the drop in ticket sales can be partly attributed to external factors, there are also internal problems that can be addressed and resolved.

The recommendations of the report are as follows:

- investigate why the premium seats check-in times increased and consider reverting to previous requirements.
- resolve dispute with cabin crew regarding working hours.
- offer more cut-price tickets.
- increase Internet presence by marketing online, and invest in making company website more user-friendly.
- target large financial institutions to market premium fares by negotiating agreements with them to handle all their air travel.

Understanding

Choose the best answer to each question.

1 How much are sales down on premium seats over the period June to December 2011?

   A 4%   √**B** 18%   **C** 20%

2 Which two groups were the focus of market research?

   √ **A** business customers and the main competitors
      B cabin crew and business customers
      (**C**) previous customers and existing customers

3 Why are business customers unhappy?

      A Because of an unresolved dispute surrounding working hours.
  √ **B** Because check-in time requirements have increased.
      C Because they are being booked into economy class instead.

4 What recommendations are made regarding FlySky Airlines' online activity?

      A They should do more marketing on the Internet and improve their website.
      B They should offer more cut-price tickets.
      C They should resolve the dispute surrounding working hours.

5 What recommendations are made specifically to address the drop in sales of premium tickets?

      A They should market their premium tickets online and sell them directly from their website.
      B They should cut the prices of premium seats in order to tempt back previous customers who now fly economy.
  √ **C** They should revert to the old check-in time requirements for premium seats and approach financial institutions directly.

Developing your reading skills

1 **You are the CEO of FlySky Airlines and you want to action all the points made in the Recommendations section. Match the two halves of the sentences to explain the reason for each task.**

1 Try to resolve the dispute with cabin crew regarding working hours ...

2 Look into whether it would be viable to offer cut-price tickets on some of our routes ...

3 Investigate why premium seats check-in times increased and try to revert back to the old system if possible ...

4 Look into targeting large financial institutions to market our premium fares, and try to negotiate agreements with them to handle all their air travel ...

5 Look at increasing our Internet presence by marketing online and consider how we can make the company website more user-friendly ...

A ... because we are being undercut by as much as 20% by some cut-price airlines.

B ... because many of our previous business customers are now flying economy, so we need to tempt them back to premium seats.

C ... because it's leading to low morale amongst staff, which is having a knock-on effect on passengers.

D ... because our business customers are not happy with the new arrangements.

E ... because we are facing intense competition from online airlines.

2 Allocate the tasks from 'Developing your reading skills 1' to the correct member of staff.

1 Sales Director who is responsible for setting ticket prices: ....

2 Personnel Manager who deals with employee disputes: *Task 1C*

3 IT and Website Manager who designed the FlySky Airlines' website: ....

4 Marketing Director who looks at ways to create new business: ....

5 Airport Liaison Manager who ensures that airport requirements are met: ....

Language focus

1 Match the verbs used in the Recommendations part of the Executive summary with their meanings.

1 investigate (an issue)   A offer for sale

2 consider (a topic)   B think about carefully

3 resolve a dispute   C gradually make better and stronger

4 increase your presence in (an area)   D try to find out more about

5 invest in (an area)   E sort out a disagreement

6 market (a product)   F discuss

7 develop (relationships)   G raise your profile/be more active in

8 negotiate (an agreement)   H spend money on

2 Complete the sentences with the correct preposition(s).

1 This report was commissioned ...*by*.... the Sales and Marketing Director.

2 The report will advise .... how profits can be increased over the next 12 months.

3 Methods .... analysis included an investigation .... the purchasing habits of families and an examination .... the trends over the last six years.

4 Market research was carried out by an independent company .... customers, aged 40–50.

5 Results .... data analysed reveal that profits decreased .... the following reasons: ...

Review

Answer this query from your colleague: 'Have you had a chance to read that report about falling transatlantic ticket sales? What were the main recommendations?'

10 Reviewing annual reports

How to read annual reports

An annual report is a financial and narrative account of the business's activities for the 12 months preceding it and a statement of its financial position at the end of the period. The structure of annual reports will vary, but for large companies they usually contain reports by the directors, CEO, or Chairman, and financial statements: profit and loss/income statement, balance sheet and cash flow statement.

- Read the contents carefully to get the gist of what is included in the report.
- Read the reports by the senior members of the company carefully – they will usually summarize the points contained in the rest of the report.
- Skim through the rest of the report, stopping to read in detail when you come across areas that are relevant to you.
- Read graphs and charts intensively as these can offer visual clues to help you understand information in the text.

Getting started

Skim over these parts of an annual report – Contents, CEO's report and Key figures – in just two minutes. Do you think the FlySky Airlines Group has had a good year? Why/Why not?

Contents

CEO's report

FlySky Airlines Group has reported a strong result amidst significant external and operational challenges in the year.

All subsidiaries of FlySky Airlines Group were profitable in spite of a series of natural disasters and spiralling fuel prices. At group level, we have seen increased revenue on last year of 6.3% and increased profit after tax of 8.2%.

A

Profit before tax:	$329 million
Profit after tax:	$198 million
Operating cash flow:	$0.9 billion
Cash held:	$1.9 billion
Revenue growth:	6%

B

We invested in three new Airbus 345s and refitted 24 of our Boeing 747 aircraft. We also extended our network with the introduction of services to Barcelona and Madrid in September.

C

Deborah Chirrey was appointed CEO in March following the retirement of Fabrice Henry. On behalf of the Board of Directors, I would like to thank Fabrice Henry for his 23 years of service to FlySky Airlines, including 12 as CEO. His legacy on the business will be lasting. Deborah Chirrey brings with her over 25 years of experience in the aviation industry, most recently as a director at Executive Airways.

We recruited new flight directors and cabin crew to cover the new routes and aircraft, bringing our total number of employees to 25,612.

D

Based on retained earnings and this year's financial result, the Board of Directors has proposed a final dividend for the year of $9.20 per share (total $4.6 million). This has been approved by the Board of Directors and is subject to the approval of shareholders at the Annual General Meeting.

E

There is a challenging year ahead, but we expect capacity and yield to increase during the first half of next year. However, fuel costs are also expected to rise, and so this will continue to put pressure on our cost base and operating margins.

With a high degree of global financial uncertainty, our main goal will be to manage our capital effectively, allocating funds to low-risk areas that produce consistent returns.

Key figures

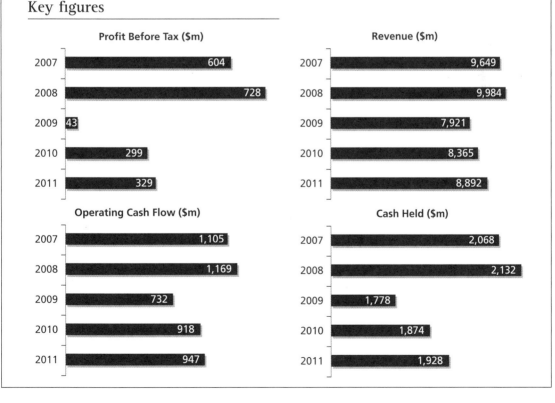

Profit Before Tax ($m)

Year	Value
2007	604
2008	728
2009	43
2010	299
2011	329

Revenue ($m)

Year	Value
2007	9,649
2008	9,984
2009	7,921
2010	8,365
2011	8,892

Operating Cash Flow ($m)

Year	Value
2007	1,105
2008	1,169
2009	732
2010	918
2011	947

Cash Held ($m)

Year	Value
2007	2,068
2008	2,132
2009	1,778
2010	1,874
2011	1,928

Understanding

Insert these missing headings next to A, B, C, D, and E in the CEO's report.

1 Dividend

4 Outlook

2 Investment in people

5 Investment in products and services

3 Financial summary

Developing your reading skills

1 Use the contents list to find the page(s) of the report you would turn to if you wanted to find the following information.

1 Information about how the company is offsetting its carbon footprint for this year.
page 16

2 Information about the aircraft.

3 The important dates for the company in the year ahead.

4 Charts showing the company's financial performance this year.

5 Reports written by the most senior employees of the company.

6 Details about charitable work done by the company.

2 Look carefully at the bar charts from the Key figures section and use the prompts to write sentences, comparing the results in different areas from year to year.

1 cash held 2007/2011
There was a higher level of cash held in 2007 than in 2011.

2 revenue 2009/2011

3 operating cash flow 2009/2011

4 profit before tax 2007/2008

5 revenue 2008/2011

6 cash held 2009/2011

7 profit before tax 2011/2009

3 You've been headhunted for a senior position at FlySky Airlines and have read their annual report to find out more about the state of the company. Are they a company that you would consider joining at the moment? Why/Why not?

....

....

....

Language focus

1 Match the terms with their meanings.

1	profit before tax	A	the amount of money that a business keeps
2	profit after tax	B	the return made by a business after operating costs have been deducted, but before tax has been charged
3	operating cash flow		
4	cash held		
5	revenue	C	the income of a business on its main activities
		D	the return made by a business after operating costs and tax have been deducted
		E	the amount of money that a business generates from its main activities

2 Insert the words from the box into the blanks.

dividend	capacity	yield/return	margin	capital

1 The .... describes the money you get from an investment.

2 .... describes the amount of cash and other assets owned by a business.

3 A .... is a portion of a company's profits, paid out to shareholders.

4 The .... of a business describes the maximum amount it can produce.

5 The .... describes the difference between the cost of a product/service and how much it is sold for.

3 Fill the blanks with the correct preposition(s).

1 FlyQuick is a subsidiary ...*of*... FlySky Airlines.

2 We saw an increase .... revenue last year .... 15%.

3 Online competitors are putting pressure .... us to offer more cut-price fares.

4 We will allocate funds .... areas of business offering the best return.

5 There's a high degree .... uncertainty regarding the coming few months.

Review

You work for Executive Airways, one of FlySky Airlines' main competitors. Your manager has asked you to read their annual report and feed back on what sort of year they've had.

11 Browsing advertisements

How to read advertisements

Advertisements are a useful source of information, which you will come across in print and online. Remember, however, that advertisements will contain a mixture of facts and opinions and that you need to be able to tell the difference between the two.

- Scan over advertisements to find any that interest you, then read these intensively for detail.
- Read with a degree of cynicism, picking out the facts where possible, but not necessarily believing all the claims that may be made.

Getting started

While flicking through your trade magazine, you see the advertisements shown on the opposite page. You have money left in your budget and are interested in:

- upgrading the employee business mobile phones
- a management course for your senior managers
- a team bonding away-day.

Scan over the advertisements in just 60 seconds – which one might be of interest to you?

Understanding

Choose the best definition for the work that each advertiser does.

1   Patel Ballard Executive Recruitment Consultants
    A A company that recruits senior to mid-level managers.
    B A blue-chip organization that provides a service that is second to none.
    C A global company with specialized industry researchers.

2   Simenons Software Solutions
    A An IT company that manufactures computers.
    B An award-winning business that provides computer support.
    C An IT company that designs or customizes software to meet client requirements.

3   Harrison and Evans School of Management
    A A legal company that provides management courses.
    B A company offering management training courses.
    C A school that offers courses in a range of subjects.

4   Strategia
    A A new business magazine.
    B A new company specialized in helping other businesses through the recession.
    C A company providing guidance on personal finance issues.

1

PATEL BALLARD

EXECUTIVE RECRUITMENT CONSULTANTS

EXCEED EXPECTATIONS

Our business is to find high-calibre professionals that will be a good fit to join your organization.

- ✔ We operate globally, recruiting for senior to mid-management positions in core industry sectors and a number of blue-chip organizations.
- ✔ Specialized industry researchers advise our consultants and help them to meet all your requirements.
- ✔ Our reputation is such that we are the first port of call for executives looking for their next move, and we provide a top-quality service that is second to none.

Don't take our word for it. To read testimonials from employers and employees, go to www.patelballardexec.com

2

Bespoke **Software Design** and **Custom Software Development** for all your IT needs.

SOFTWARE

SIMENONS

SOLUTIONS

Awarded Badge of Excellence by Business Services Inc.
www.simenons.com

Excellence
BUSINESS SERVICING

3

Harrison and Evans School of Management

TURN YOUR MANAGERS INTO LEADERS

❝ Before I went on a Harrison and Evans management course, I used to get caught up in the day-to-day detail of office life. But this course was ideal for me because it showed me how to look at the big picture, which has allowed me to think more strategically about my business. ❞

Douglas Peterson, Senior Legal Adviser
Clarks and Kays Solicitors

Douglas attended our *Strategic Thinking for the Future* course.

Let us help you develop, improve and meet your full potential.

There are over 50 management and leadership courses available, so we are sure to have one that fits your requirements! With 37 years of experience, we only use highly qualified instructors who teach in small groups.

You can download a brochure from www.harrisonevans.com or call us on 02933 299 388

4

STRATEGIA

Save up to **25%** by taking out your subscription early at www.strategia.com Online and app edition also available.

A new business magazine, launched to help you navigate your way through the stormy seas of economic recession.

From next month, look out for it on your newsstands:

- expert analysis of business news
- global economic forecasts
- detailed commentary on latest technology, energy, and industry trends and developments
- essential reports on market movements
- in-depth company profiles
- valuable investment ideas
- professional guidance on personal finance issues

Developing your reading skills

1 You are interested in finding out particular pieces of information about the advertisers. Scan over the advertisements and decide if the following details are included or not.

Information	Included	Not included
1 Information about the types of companies that Patel Ballard Executive Recruitment Consultants work with.	✓	
2 Names of the companies that Patel Ballard Executive Recruitment Consultants work with.		
3 A detailed breakdown of all services provided by Simenons Software Solutions.		
4 Details about the cost of Harrison and Evans School of Management courses.		
5 A detailed breakdown of the types of article that will be appearing in *Strategia*.		
6 A website link for readers to get a special discount by subscribing early to *Strategia*.		

2 When reading advertisements, you must distinguish between information (details that you can check are true or not) and opinion (somebody's viewpoint that may or may not be true). Decide whether the following extracts contain information or opinion.

From advertisement 1:

1 We provide a top-quality service that is second to none.
   Information   (Opinion)
2 To read testimonials from employers and employees, go to www.patelballardexec.com.
   Information   Opinion

From advertisement 2:

3 Awarded Badge of Excellence by Business Services Inc.
   Information   Opinion

From advertisement 3:

4 There are over 50 management and leadership courses available.
   Information   Opinion
5 We are sure to have one that fits your requirements!
   Information   Opinion
6 You can download a brochure from www.harrisonevans.com or call us on 02933 299 388.
   Information   Opinion

From advertisement 4:

7 valuable investment ideas
   Information   Opinion
8 Online and app edition also available.
   Information   Opinion

Language focus

1 Match the adjectives with their meanings.

1	expert	A	concerning or including the whole world
2	in-depth	B	useful or worth a lot of money
3	global	C	absolutely necessary
4	essential	D	skilful/knowledgeable
5	valuable	E	of good quality
6	specialized	F	thorough/in a lot of detail
7	high-calibre	G	developed for a particular purpose

2 Insert the missing prepositions into these idioms from the advertisements.

1 get caught up ...*in*... something
2 look .... the big picture
3 be a good fit .... something
4 first port .... call
5 second .... none
6 take somebody's word .... it

3 Rewrite these sentences replacing the underlined sections with one of the idioms from 'Language Focus 2'.

1 This new updated software is <u>better than any other software</u>.
   This new updated software is second to none. ....

2 We're thinking too much about the detail – we need to <u>consider the broad overall view of the issue</u>.
   ....

3 <u>Trust me</u> – our product is superior to those of our competitors.
   ....

4 Thanks to our new marketing campaign, we have become the <u>first place that people come</u> for online computer support.
   ....

5 We've <u>become involved in</u> a legal battle that we didn't want.
   ....

6 We're delighted with the new CEO – he seems to <u>suit our company very well</u>.
   ....

Review

Scan through a trade publication or business newspaper and circle five advertisements for products or services that you might be interested in. Read them intensively, underlining any sections that you think are 'opinion' rather than 'information'. Underline any vocabulary that describes the product in an attractive way. Are you tempted to purchase any of the products/services? Why/Why not?

Product and service brochures

How to read product and service brochures

Product and service brochures are created in order to promote businesses and what they do. They can be a good source of information, but remember that they are promotional tools and can include opinions as well as facts.

- Skim through a brochure to get a general impression of the company.
- Scan over it to find sections of interest to you before reading them intensively.
- Read with an awareness that the text will be biased to highlight the features and benefits of the product/service, and will not mention any potential drawbacks.

Getting started

1 **What do you look for in a product or service brochure? Tick the options that you think should be included.**

1 A well-presented overview of what the business does.
2 Details about the company's history and working practices.
3 Pictures or photographs to illustrate the product or service supplied.
4 An organigram of the business.
5 A detailed breakdown of the products or service.
6 Details about the cost of the products or service.
7 Details about the conditions attached to products and services.

2 **A service brochure has landed on your desk. Scan over the contents list below and answer these questions. Then read the brochure extract.**

1 What sort of business is Kaymans Inc.?

....

2 Do they provide a business service? If so, what page do you need to turn to find out more?

....

CONTENTS

Kaymans Inc.

BUSINESS HEALTHCARE

KEEP YOUR BUSINESS IN GOOD HEALTH

- **Cut the cost of sick days**
A recent survey has shown that a staggering 180 million working days are lost each year due to sickness, at a cost of over £16.8 billion to British business (which equates to £595 per employee).* Kaymans Inc. healthcare will cut this cost for you – regular employee health checkups may prevent days lost to sickness and when an employee does fall ill, timely high-quality medical care will ensure that they are absent for as short a time as possible.

- **Make yourself a more attractive employer**
A Kaymans Inc. healthcare package can help you to attract the very best employees and retain a happy healthy workforce who perceive that their employer cares about their welfare.

WHY CHOOSE KAYMANS INC.?

- Flexible cover allows you to choose a personalized scheme to meet the requirements of your policyholders.

- Services available to suit large or small businesses.

- Prompt reliable medical service from experienced healthcare providers and a 24-hour health helpline.

- Speedy appointments designed to fit around working hours.

- Access to 250 high-quality hospitals and 750 experienced consultants.

- Peace of mind that comes from choosing a health insurer with over 50 years of experience.

DESIGNING MY KAYMANS INC. PACKAGE

- **The core package**
This contains various types of hospital cover (out-patient, day-patient, in-patient), a private ambulance and access to our 24-hour health helpline.

- **Additional options**
You can set the level of hospital cover that you choose to provide; you can add in a members' excess option (where employees contribute towards their treatment); you can add dental care, optical care, and psychiatric cover.

- **Skilled advice and guidance**
Our advisers will be able to help you choose the package that suits you and your company best, based on where you are located and the needs of your employees.

12

Understanding

Are the following statements True or False? Correct any that are false.

1 Kaymans Inc. offers a range of services: personal health insurance, business health insurance, home insurance, and car insurance.

....

2 The brochure claims that Kaymans Inc. cover can make your company more attractive for prospective employees.

....

3 Kaymans Inc. only supplies health cover for large and medium-sized companies.

....

4 Kaymans Inc. cover can be tailored to the needs of individuals.

....

5 The basic package covers hospital visits, transportation to and from the hospital, and a 24-hour health helpline.

....

6 Psychiatric cover is not offered by Kaymans Inc.

....

Developing your reading skills

1 You are interested in adding private healthcare to your company's employee benefit package. You run a small business with 48 employees and want a flexible scheme with the option of dental and optical cover. You've had problems in the past with insurers who have gone out of business so you're looking for a long-standing secure healthcare provider.

Scan over the extract from the brochure. Find three things which show that Kaymans Inc. meets your requirements.

....

....

....

2 Read these extracts from the brochure with a sceptical eye. Tick the statements that you believe to be true (facts) and put a question mark next to those that you are not convinced about (opinions).

1 Kaymans Inc. healthcare will cut this cost [of sick days] for you. **?**

2 A Kaymans Inc. healthcare package can help you to attract the very best employees.

3 A Kaymans Inc. healthcare package can help you to retain a happy healthy workforce who perceive that their employer cares about their welfare.

4 The Kaymans Inc. basic healthcare package offers a 24-hour health helpline.

5 Kaymans Inc. offers access to 750 experienced consultants.

6 You can add dental care, optical care and psychiatric cover.

Language focus

1 Match the adjectives with their meanings.

1	high-quality	A	made for a particular individual
2	flexible	B	with the knowledge and ability to do something well
3	personalized	C	superior/excellent/of a very good standard
4	prompt	D	done without delay
5	reliable	E	trustworthy/accurate
6	skilled	F	able to change and adapt easily to different conditions

2 Complete the sentences with the correct preposition.

1 The product cost is based ....*on*......... the quantity ordered.
2 It's suitable .... large or small businesses.
3 With this service, you get access .... a wealth of information and experience.
4 This service is available at a cost .... £300/month.
5 With over 45 years .... experience, our service is reliable and trustworthy.

3 Complete the sentences with the words and phrases from the box below, which relate to business healthcare insurance.

healthcare provider	core package	sick day	excess	flexible cover	policyholder

1 A .... is an organization that supplies medical treatment to its members.
2 When an employee is too unwell to come to work, they take a ....
3 A .... is a person covered by an insurance contract.
4 An .... is a set contribution paid by the policyholder towards the cost of the insurance.
5 If you can design an insurance policy to fit your needs, you have ....
6 The .... is the basic set of services that are provided in an insurance policy.

Review

Your boss asks you to look into the Kaymans Inc. business package and summarize the main features of the service. What do you say to your boss?

13 Exploring company websites

Getting started

You work for Kaymans Inc. and your boss has asked you to check out the website of RSL, a health insurance company, which is one of your main competitors. You type 'RSL' into your search engine and it returns the following results. Which would you click on to find the company website that you are looking for? Then study the web page opposite.

1 RSL, Royal Society of Lifeguards

   www.royallifeguardsociety.org

2 Run Swim Live, RSL health club

   www.runswimlive.com

3 Resin Supplies Ltd, official website for all your resin needs ...

   www.resinsupplies.com

4 Register of Social Landlords – The Scottish Housing Regulator, RSL ...

   www.esystems.scottishhousingregulator.gov.uk/.../reg_pub_dsp.hom.

5 Raymonds, Simon and Landsdowne – official website of healthcare provider, RSL

   www.rslhealth.com

6 RSL, Reinsurance Summaries Ltd, specialists in reinsurance services ...

   www.rslinsurers.com

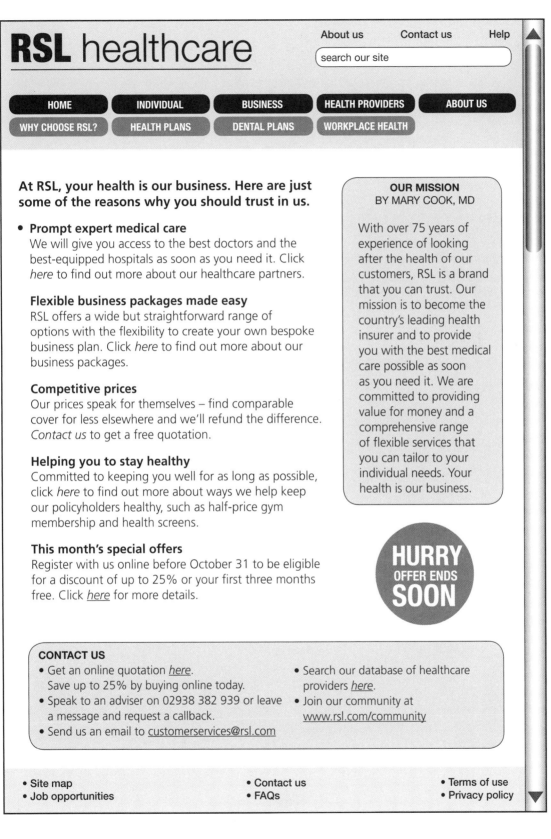

RSL healthcare

About us   Contact us   Help

search our site

HOME   **INDIVIDUAL**   **BUSINESS**   **HEALTH PROVIDERS**   **ABOUT US**

WHY CHOOSE RSL?   **HEALTH PLANS**   **DENTAL PLANS**   **WORKPLACE HEALTH**

At RSL, your health is our business. Here are just some of the reasons why you should trust in us.

- **Prompt expert medical care**
  We will give you access to the best doctors and the best-equipped hospitals as soon as you need it. Click *here* to find out more about our healthcare partners.

  Flexible business packages made easy
  RSL offers a wide but straightforward range of options with the flexibility to create your own bespoke business plan. Click *here* to find out more about our business packages.

  Competitive prices
  Our prices speak for themselves – find comparable cover for less elsewhere and we'll refund the difference. *Contact us* to get a free quotation.

  Helping you to stay healthy
  Committed to keeping you well for as long as possible, click *here* to find out more about ways we help keep our policyholders healthy, such as half-price gym membership and health screens.

  This month's special offers
  Register with us online before October 31 to be eligible for a discount of up to 25% or your first three months free. Click *here* for more details.

OUR MISSION
BY MARY COOK, MD

With over 75 years of experience of looking after the health of our customers, RSL is a brand that you can trust. Our mission is to become the country's leading health insurer and to provide you with the best medical care possible as soon as you need it. We are committed to providing value for money and a comprehensive range of flexible services that you can tailor to your individual needs. Your health is our business.

HURRY OFFER ENDS SOON

CONTACT US
- Get an online quotation *here*.
  Save up to 25% by buying online today.
- Speak to an adviser on 02938 382 939 or leave a message and request a callback.
- Send us an email to customerservices@rsl.com
- Search our database of healthcare providers *here*.
- Join our community at www.rsl.com/community

- Site map
- Job opportunities
- Contact us
- FAQs
- Terms of use
- Privacy policy

Understanding

Your boss has asked you to find out the methods that RSL Healthcare is using to try to persuade new customers to sign up. Read the website again and make notes about four relevant benefits or promotions.

> • *Customers are given prompt access to the best doctors and best-equipped hospitals.*
> • ....
> • ....
> • ....
> • ....

Developing your reading skills

Which of the links in the box would you click on in these situations?

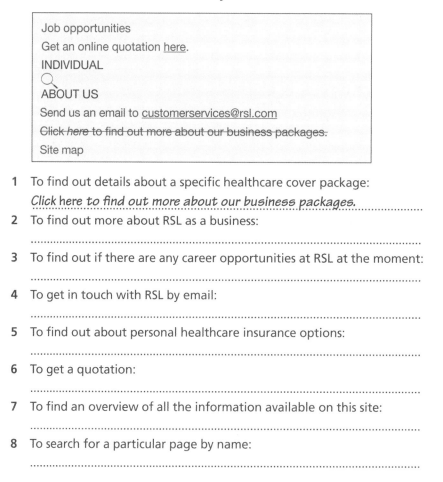

Job opportunities

Get an online quotation here.

INDIVIDUAL

ABOUT US

Send us an email to customerservices@rsl.com

~~Click *here* to find out more about our business packages.~~

Site map

1 To find out details about a specific healthcare cover package:
   Click here to find out more about our business packages.

2 To find out more about RSL as a business:
   ....

3 To find out if there are any career opportunities at RSL at the moment:
   ....

4 To get in touch with RSL by email:
   ....

5 To find out about personal healthcare insurance options:
   ....

6 To get a quotation:
   ....

7 To find an overview of all the information available on this site:
   ....

8 To search for a particular page by name:
   ....

Language focus

1 Choose the word or phrase from the box which relates to the definitions below.

Log in	Help	Contact us	Site map	Terms of use
Register	About us	FAQs	Job opportunities	Privacy policy

1 Frequently asked questions – a list of commonly asked questions and their answers.
FAQs...

2 A page to tell you more about the organization.
....

3 A page where you enter your personal details and give a username and password the first time that you use the website services.
....

4 A page to give you all the information you need to get in touch with the company, for example, its address, email address, and telephone number.
....

5 A page to enter your username and password so you can use the website again.
....

6 A page that lists jobs which are currently available in the organization.
....

7 A page that sets out how the organization will use the personal information that you give them on the website.
....

8 A page that will help you if you are stuck.
....

9 A page to give an overview of the information on the website to help you find what you are looking for.
....

10 A page to show the legal agreement between you and the service provider.
....

2 Match the beginnings and ends of the sentences.

1	Get an ...	A	community at www.webcommunity.com.
2	Speak to an ...	B	comparable product for less elsewhere and we'll refund the difference.
3	Send us ...	C	our database of products and services.
4	Search ...	D	adviser on 0938227388.
5	Join our ...	E	before October 31 to be eligible for a discount of up to 25%.
6	Find a ...	F	an email to customers@web.com.
7	Register with us ...	G	online quotation here.

Review

Go online and explore the websites of three or four of your major competitors. Consider how they present and promote their products/services, and how these compare to those of your own business. What special promotions are they offering?

Social media

How to read social media and Twitter

Marketing business online is big business. Many companies now exploit different forms of social media, such as social networking sites, blogs, or Twitter as a way of creating a buzz about new developments within the business or the launch of new products or services.

- Scan through social media updates from companies related to yours to find out about the latest developments within their businesses – breaking news is sometimes released online before it is made public through the usual channels.

- Do not be lulled into a false sense of security by the informal setting of the Internet – remember that you are still reading promotional material, so read it with the same degree of cynicism as you would an advertisement, company brochure, or company website.

Getting started

Scan over the social networking site and Twitter page in just 30 seconds. What topic is being widely talked about today?

WORLD CONNECTIONS
SWALLOWS Electronics manufacturer

Search 🔍

👍 Like

Share ◁ Write here ...

Swallows
Only 3 days to go now till the launch of the hotly anticipated Swallows Tablet. Have you pre-ordered yours yet? For more information go to www.swallows.co.uk/tablet. And for exclusive pictures, like this page!

Like • Comment • Share

👍 **566 people like this**

Max Tucker I can't wait!! I've been wanting one of these for ages!

Leila Girling Why all the fuss?? Aren't there enough tablets out there already?!

Swallows
We are proud to announce that we are the official sponsors of the FA Cup this year! Which teams would you like to see playing each other?

Like • Comment • Share

👍 **1,147 people like this**

Swallows
Swallows customer review, from Gracie 67 on our new laptop 600: 'This is such a great laptop, I just love it! The screen is so clear and crisp and you can see every detail even when watching movies!' For more customer reviews, go to: www.swallows.co.uk/customerfeedback.

SWALLOWS
Computers

Wall

Info

Home

About

549,000
people like this
642
people are
talking about this

Likes 👍

Swallows
International

Swallows
Customer
Group

Home   @Connect   #Discover   Search

Swallowstablet
View my profile page

806	21138	18566
TWEETS	FOLLOWNG	FOLLOWERS

Compose new Tweet

Who to follow • Refresh • View all

CollinsELT@CollinsELT   x

Collins Language
@CollinsLanguage   x

Punctuation Panda   x
@PunchyPanda

Worldwide trends • Change

#favefilmfever
#newSwallowstablet
#overeating
Brian Mann
Samba
Hello Dolly
Ivy Harris
Happy birthday Pedro Mariotti
Lunar eclipse
Kay SFV

twitter

© 2012 Twitter About Help Terms Privacy
Blog Status Apps Resources Jobs
Advertisers Businesses Media Developers

Tweets

Swallow   2m
For exclusive pictures of #newSwallowsTablet
go to worldconnections.co.uk/swallowscomps and
like our homepage.

Swallow   3m
#newSwallowsTablet To read the latest product
development blog, go to
www.swallows.co.uk/tablet/developmentblog.

Gordonowash   1h
#newSwallowsTablet I've always preferred Laks
Computers to Swallows ... much more reliable.

tablet4business   2h
Read our review of the #newSwallowsTablet in next
month's edition. It seems to tick all the right boxes for a
business tablet ...
↺ Retweeted by SwallowsOfficial

pete_hammAUS   2h
What's this #newSwallowsTablet that's trending?????
Haven't heard anything about it in Australia!

Swallowsfan34   3h
DM SwallowsOfficial I'm seriously excited about the
new tablet #newSwallowsTablet....only three days to
go now!!!
↺ Retweeted by SwallowsOfficial

Swallow   3h
@conterifiraldi Thanks for your question! For a
list of all our commercial suppliers worldwide,
go to www.swallows.co.uk/suppliers.

Swallow   3h
We've got #newSwallowsTablet trending worldwide!
Thank you tweeple! To pre-order go to
www.swallows.co.uk/tablet.

conterifiraldi   3h
Does anyone know where I'll be able to buy the
#newSwallowsTablet in Italy??? Don't want to have to
wait for delivery by ordering online ...

Understanding

Are the following statements True or False? Correct any that are false.

1   Swallows are promoting the launch of their new laptop on World Connections, a social networking site.

....

2   Swallows have used the social networking site to announce the fact that they are sponsoring a sports event.

....

3   Gracie 67 is very satisfied with her new Swallows Laptop 600.

....

4   Lots of people on Twitter are discussing the launch of the new Swallows Tablet.

....

5   Conterifiraldi wants to know where he or she can buy the Swallows Tablet in Spain.

....

6   Gordonowash is likely to buy the new Swallows Tablet.

....

Developing your reading skills

1   Read the comments or Tweets made by the following people. Do they like or dislike Swallows Computers? Circle the best option.

1	Max Tucker	(Like)	Dislike	Don't know
2	Leila Girling	Like	Dislike	Don't know
3	Gracie 67	Like	Dislike	Don't know
4	conterifiraldi	Like	Dislike	Don't know
5	Gordonowash	Like	Dislike	Don't know
6	pete_hammAUS	Like	Dislike	Don't know

2   Analyse how Swallows promotes their product launch on Twitter and tick the strategies that they use below.

1   They are encouraging people to talk about it in order to get the subject trending worldwide, which will mean that more people hear about it. ✓

2   They are responding to individual readers' questions.

3   They are providing links to their company website where people can order the Tablet.

4   They are talking about all its unique features.

5   They are providing links to the product development blog.

6   They are describing why the Swallows Tablet is better than the competition.

7   They are retweeting any Tweets that speak favourably about the Swallows Tablet.

8   They are providing links to the latest music releases.

Language focus

1 Match the common terms from social networking sites with their meanings.

1 post on a wall   A show your approval of something on a social networking site

2 share a comment   B leave a message on somebody's homepage

3 like something 👍   C respond publicly to something on a social networking site

4 show up in a timeline   D appear in a sequence of messages in chronological order, with the most recent at the top

2 Complete the sentences with the words and phrases from the box.

to Tweet	Tweets	Tweeters/Twitterers/Tweeple	to follow them	followers

1 If you sign up to receive a person's messages in your timeline, then you are said ....

2 People who post messages on Twitter are known as ....

3 The short 140-character-only messages on Twitter are called ....

4 People who receive your messages are known as your ....

5 If you post a message on Twitter, then you are said ....

3 Match these unique Twitter features to their explanations.

1 DM SwallowsOfficial @conterifiraldi   A Two ways of reposting (or repeating) something that has already been said by another Twitterer.

2 ↻ Retweeted by SwallowsOfficial   B Topics that are being discussed by lots of users are said to be 'trending' and a list of current trending topics is visible on your homepage. Users tag their Tweets with a hashtag to link it to the debate.

3 trending worldwide #newSwallowsTablet

   C Two ways of sending somebody a personal message on Twitter. 'DM' is a direct message and will be seen only by the named follower. '@' replies will appear in the person's timeline and can be seen by other users too.

Review

Go online and investigate how active your main competitors are at promoting their products online. Like their pages on social networking sites and follow them on Twitter so that you receive regular updates about special promotions or new product/service launches that they may be planning. Analyse the messages that they post and relationships that they have with their customers.

15 Reading the news

How to read newspaper reports

The business pages of newspapers and online news websites are a useful source of information about global issues that might affect your work. News articles are usually set out in the same way: the headline is a short attention-grabbing summary of the story, designed to hook readers and make them want to read on; the first paragraph is usually a brief summary of the story; and the rest of the article examines the story in depth.

- Scan over the headlines of the business pages to find an article of interest.
- Then read over the first paragraph and skim through the rest of the article for a summary of the story.
- If it is a story that interests you, read it extensively for general understanding.
- Look out for language that indicates a political bias on the part of the writer.

Getting started

Study the headline below and predict which of the three sentences best describes what the article is about. Then read the introduction and first paragraph of the article on the page opposite to see if you were right.

1 The gulf between rich and poor is fundamental to the survival of capitalist society.
2 The gulf between rich and poor could be dangerous for capitalist society.
3 Capitalist society is dead.

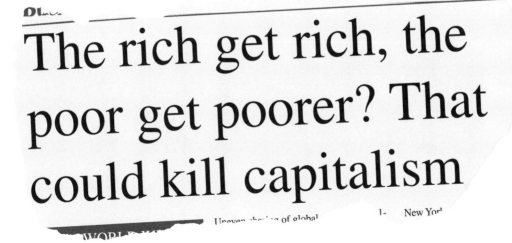

Uneven sharing of global wealth could undermine the entire capitalist system the World Economic Forum was told yesterday.

There is a growing feeling among political leaders in Davos that change is needed. In particular, pay and rewards cannot disproportionately flow to the already rich.

Nouriel Roubini, who was speaking on the future of capitalism, warned that financial and social imbalances could trigger unrest.

Mr Roubini was nicknamed Doctor Doom after he highlighted the excesses in the financial system before the crash.

He said: 'The 1920s were a gilded age but there was also rising inequality. Then we had the crash, and a range of policy responses led to the Great Depression. We then had the rise of the authoritarian regimes and we ended up with World War Two. I'm not saying that is going to happen again but if we don't relieve the financial, fiscal and social problems that exist there are risks for the future.'

There has already been unrest in European countries after austerity measures, and "occupy" protests in New York and London against capitalism.

Lael Brainard, US Undersecretary of the Treasury, said: 'Leading up to the crisis we saw a disproportionate share of wealth going to the richest, and changes to the tax system reinforced that. We need to turn that around.'

Much criticism of excessive rewards has been directed at bankers, who are frequently blamed for causing the financial crisis that pushed countries into recession.

Angel Gurría, Secretary General of the OECD, said: 'I think compensation is one of the problems [that creates inequality]. This is one of the things that brought about the crisis: unrelenting greed. It is happening again.'

Mr Roubini said: 'There has been a massive increase in wealth in the past decade and also an increase in inequalities. We are also now seeing this rising inequality in China and other emerging economies that will be a problem.

Even after the crisis there is certainly a perception that nothing has changed. In good times there were profits, risks were taken and excessive rewards earned. In the bad times the losses were put on the balance sheets of governments and that created the massive sovereign debt problems.'

The participants in the Davos debate called for an injection of morality into the capitalist system and for businessmen and companies to act in the interests of broader society.

Anders Borg, Sweden's finance minister, said: 'If profits are taken out of Swedish society and put in some Channel Island to avoid tax, that is bad. Profits invested to create jobs is good for society. Companies must see the moral difference. The business world must behave in a more moral way.'

David Robertson

Adapted from an article in *The Times*.

Understanding

Are the following statements True or False? Correct any that are false.

1   Political leaders in Davos have warned that the inequality between rich and poor could lead to social unrest.

   ....

2   Nouriel Roubini was nicknamed Doctor Doom because he said that a financial crash would never happen.

   ....

3   Mr Roubini draws on examples from history to make his point.

   ....

4   Lael Brainard believes that the tax system went some way to close the gap between the rich and the poor.

   ....

5   Mr Roubini thinks that inequality between rich and poor is only a problem in the West.

   ....

6   Anders Borg believes that business people need to be more moral.

   ....

Developing your reading skills

1   Is the journalist presenting a balanced debate on the subject 'The rich get rich, the poor get poorer? That could kill capitalism' or is he writing from one point of view only? To help you answer this question, decide whether the following contributors agree or disagree with the statement.

1   Nouriel Roubini   Agree / Disagree
2   Lael Brainard   Agree / Disagree
3   Angel Gurría   Agree / Disagree
4   Anders Borg   Agree / Disagree

2   Summarize the main point made by each contributor using your own words.

Contributor	Argument
Nouriel Roubini	*Financial and social imbalances could lead to unrest – we should learn lessons from history, e.g. the boom of the 1920s, followed by the Great Depression led to World War Two.*
Lael Brainard	
Angel Gurría	
Anders Borg	

Language focus

1 Group these words and phrases under the correct heading.

| austerity measures | crash | wealth | financial crisis | gilded age |
| profits | losses | recession | rewards | sovereign debt problems |

Words related to economic 'good times'	Words related to economic 'bad times'
	austerity measures

2 Match the verbs with their meanings.

1 undermine (line 2)   A alleviate/lessen the pain of something
2 flow (line 9)   B make something less certain or secure
3 trigger (line 14)   C draw attention to something
4 highlight (line 16)   D make something stronger/boost
5 relieve (line 26)   E move freely
6 reinforce (line 39)   F set off/cause something to happen

3 Complete the sentences with the correct preposition.

1 The CEO spoke *on/about* the future of the company.
2 The shareholders called .... an additional meeting on the subject.
3 The criticism was directed .... the Chairman.
4 There was some uncertainty leading up .... the Annual General Meeting.
5 This decision will bring .... many job losses.
6 We are acting .... the interests of our clients.
7 The current financial crisis is to blame .... our falling profits.
8 Our competitors have behaved .... a most unprofessional manner.

4 Complete the sentences with a suitable adjective from the box.

| emerging | excessive | disproportionate | rising |

1 It's unfair that a .... share of wealth goes to the rich.
2 I think that bankers earn too much money – they receive .... rewards for the job that they do.
3 There's .... inequality here too – it's been increasing for the last 10 years.
4 An .... economy is described as one with low to middle per capita income.

Review

Your colleague has also read the article on page 61. Respond to her question: 'Do you agree that businesspeople need to behave in a more moral way for the sake of capitalism?' Give your personal opinion.

16 Business media websites

Getting started

 Tick the statements that you agree with.

1 I prefer to read newspapers because there's always so much information on business media websites that I find it hard to focus on stories of interest.

2 I prefer business media websites because they are updated throughout the day. The problem with newspapers is that they are already out of date by the time you hold them in your hands.

3 I find print journalism more reliable and trustworthy than online journalism because it is subject to tighter controls.

4 Business media websites are much more convenient – all the information you need is at your fingertips. And it's often provided for free.

2 **Your boss has just told you that your company is interested in investing in projects in Vietnam this year. Scan over the business media homepage again and decide which two stories you would read in more detail.**

1 ....

2 ....

BUSINESS LINE

About us   Contact us   Help

search our site

BREAKING NEWS   See all

10.18 Gold falls on yen strength, lower stocks
10.06 Euro down amidst more crisis talks
09.58 Technical problems with 3G phone hit Swallows International stocks
09.32 Yesterday's biggest gains and falls
09.18 Kays Manufacturing shares drop 4% following CEO's resignation

More markets and currency rates

MARKETS

DOW JONES	12,349	−23.12 ▼
FTSE	5,229	−12.40 ▼
NIKKEI	8,459	+63.68 ▲

HOME   **BUSINESS**   **ECONOMY**   **MARKETS**   **INVESTMENTS**   **MONEY**

FEATURES AND ANALYSIS

Haymans and Sons to float
Leading pharmaceutical company is to go public in September in a move that is thought to be worth $3 billion to the owners.

Girling Hamilton and J Regan Motors in $8 billion merger
The car manufacturer Girling Hamilton formally announced plans to merge with J Regan Motors in a deal that will give the combined new business a total value of $8 billion.

US bank pushes for Vietnam infrastructure deals
American bank Portman & Sons are set to play an important role in Vietnam's fast growing economy, by bidding for infrastructure deals related to satellite communication and renewable energy.

Mixed day for profit announcements
Oil company Carters Providence announced annual profits of $13.8 billion, and share prices soared, whereas Sharmans Investment Bank reported that profits were down by 48% compared to the same period last year, which led to their share prices tumbling by 12%.

MOST VIEWED   **MOST SHARED**

1 Girling Hamilton and J Regan Motors in $8 billion merger

2 Top ten tips for doing business in East Asia

3 The company that holds all meetings standing up

4 CEO of top bank to waive bonus

5 Euro set to drop further against dollar

Quick links
- Business profiles
- Business opinions
- Money guide
- Market guide

Services
- News/RSS feeds
- Podcasts
- Blogs
- Follow us on Twitter
- Like us on World Connections

- Help
- Site index
- Feedback
- Code of conduct
- Work for us

Understanding

Answer these questions.

1 What are the five main subject areas on the site, in the main header tabs?

1 .... / 2 .... / 3 .... / 4 .... / 5 ....

2 What's the most recent article of breaking news?

....

3 What's the story that has been read the most number of times today?

....

4 Details about which three markets feature on the webpage?

1 .... / 2 .... / 3 ....

5 What's the best description of the types of story covered on this website?

A The latest advice on personal finance

B Everything you need to know about setting up your own business

C The latest news about the markets and major businesses

Developing your reading skills

1 **Which links would you click to find out more about …**

1 … the performance of the FTSE?   *More markets and currency rates*

2 … advice on personal finance?   ....

3 … how the Euro is performing against the dollar?   ....

4 … all the breaking news from today?   ....

5 … the story about a CEO refusing his bonus?   ....

6 … the merger between two big car manufacturers?   ....

7 … jobs available at the organization?   ....

8 … Carters Providence oil company?   ....

2 **You get a call from a colleague who is working from home today. He asks you: 'My Internet has gone down – can you do me a favour and check on Businessline because I need to know the latest on markets?' Scan the webpage to find answers to his questions.**

1 'What's the level of the Nikkei at the moment?'

....

2 'Any news on Swallows International stocks?'

....

3 'I heard rumours about Haymans and Sons yesterday. Any announcements from them?'

....

4 'What's going on with the euro today?'

....

5 'Has the FTSE gone up or down?'

....

6 'Has gold gone up or down?'

....

7 'What's the latest on shares in Sharmans Investment Bank?'

....

Language focus

1 Match these words and phrases with their meanings.

1 Breaking news
2 Features and analysis
3 Most viewed
4 Most shared
5 News/RSS feeds
6 Podcast
7 Blog

A a data format that enables you to see when a website has added new content, giving you access to all the latest headlines without having to visit each individual webpage

B a list of webpages that have been recommended the most often by readers to other contacts by way of social media

C a digital audio or video file that can be downloaded from the Internet, usually focusing on a particular subject area

D a webpage featuring a commentary on a particular subject or a journal

E the very latest stories that have just been published online

F a list of webpages that have been read the most often

G in-depth articles and stories

2 The grammar of headlines is different from standard written English. Match the grammar rules to their examples.

Rules:

1 Headlines do not usually contain articles.
2 Simple verbs are more common than continuous verbs.
3 The infinitive is used to refer to the future.
4 Headlines may feature noun phrases or noun strings, so you will have to work out what the verb might be.

Examples:

A Girling Hamilton and J Regan Motors in $8 billion merger
B Mixed day for profit announcements
C Haymans and Sons to float
D US bank pushes for Vietnam infrastructure deals

Review

Go online and search for business media websites. Have a look at about three or four. Compare how they present the stories of the day, and decide which you find the most user-friendly. Then check for updates every day for a week, spending just a few minutes scanning the headlines and stories of interest. If you find that you are better informed than you were before, make this a regular part of your work day.

17

Analysing the money or personal finance section

How to read the money section

The money section of newspapers or media websites provides financial advice about the most effective ways to invest capital.

- Scan over the headlines of the money section to find an article of interest and then read extensively for general understanding, taking particular note of any financial data provided.

- Remember that advice given is not necessarily true and is simply the opinion of one (or more) financial adviser(s). And predictions about future happenings are merely informed guesses and tend to have a poor track record.

- When you are skimming through a money article, use the clues in the text to help you to follow the gist of what is being said. Subheadings serve as useful summaries of each section, for example: 'The basics', 'Shares', and 'Conclusion'. The opening sentence of a paragraph (known as the topic sentence) often summarizes the rest of the paragraph, for example: 'But the tax breaks available for those who can make this lifestyle choice are considerable.' (lines 33–35). Questions posed at the beginning of a paragraph are usually answered within the paragraph, for example: 'Want to get by on dividends alone?' (line 19).

Getting started

Read the opening paragraph of the article on the opposite page and skim through the rest of the article in just two minutes. Then choose the best headline for this story.

How to prepare for retirement

How to invest capital wisely

How to live like the idle rich

BY MARK ATHERTON

INVESTMENTS Record dividends mean it is possible to lie back and watch the money roll in, says Mark Atherton.

A bumper year for share dividends lies ahead, despite a looming recession. These distributions, made by companies to their shareholders, reached a record £67.8 billion last year. A further increase is forecast for this year, as companies return rising profits to investors.

This may be good news for pension funds and individuals reliant on dividends for income, especially as once a company has raised its payout, a future cut is unlikely. But there is sure to be more criticism of this use of company funds, especially in difficult economic times.

THE BASICS

Want to get by on dividends alone? Then you need a substantial capital sum. You would, for example, require £650,000 to achieve an income of £26,000, equivalent to UK average earnings. This is based on the current yield of four per cent from shares in the FTSE 100 index.

Jonathon Jackson of Killik & Co., the stockbroker, says: 'In practice you would require more than this and you would need a cash buffer to smooth over irregular dividend payments.'

But the tax breaks available for those who can make this lifestyle choice are considerable. Chas Roy-Chowdhury of the Association of Chartered Certified Accountants says a worker on £26,000 would pay £3,705 in tax and £2,276 in national insurance – £5,981 in total. The effective tax on dividends of £26,000 would be zero, with no national insurance to pay.

You should, of course, remember that some banks abruptly stopped paying dividends after the credit crunch of 2008-9 and BP suspended its dividend.

SHARES

Jeremy Batstone-Carr, of Charles Stanley, the stockbroker, says that you would need to spend your £650,000 across at least 20 stocks to limit your risk. Mr Jackson suggests you look for 'international high-yielding stocks with strong balance sheets that look capable of sustaining good dividend payments'. To guard against excessive concentration, Mr Jackson thinks you should add stocks with more modest yields but good prospects of rapid dividend growth.

CONCLUSION

With cash deposit rates low and share yields high, investing for dividends makes a lot of financial sense – if you have the money. You may think that living off your investments is not for you, but remember that that is exactly what you, and everyone else, will effectively be doing in your retirement.

Adapted from an article in *The Times*.

Understanding

Choose the correct answer to these questions.

1 What is the main point of the article?
 A Now is a good time to invest for dividends.
 B Now is a good time to buy shares.
 C Now is a good time to spread your shares portfolio across at least 20 stocks to limit your risk.

2 How much is forecast to be paid out in dividends in the year ahead?
 A £67.8 billion   C Less than £67.8 billion
 B More than £67.8 billion

3 How much capital must be invested to earn a return in dividends equal to an average UK salary?
 A £26,000   C A minimum of £650,000
 B A maximum of £650,000

4 What point is made about retirement in the final paragraph?
 A You should invest in stocks now so that you have a high enough pension.
 B Rising dividends is good for pension funds.
 C We will all effectively have to live off our savings when we retire.

Developing your reading skills

1 Extract the three tips from the stockbrokers about the types of shares that investors should choose.

1 You should *invest across at least 20 stocks to limit your risk.* .
2 You should ....
3 You should ....

2 When reading an article, you must be able to understand references within it. Look back to the text to work out what the words in bold refer to?

1 '**This** may be good news for pension funds and individuals ...,' (line 10)
 A rising profits for next year
 B forecast increase in dividends for next year
 C the looming recession

2 '**This** is based on the current yield of four per cent from shares in the FTSE100 index.' (line 24)
 A the calculation of how much capital must be invested to yield dividends of £26,000
 B the calculation of average UK earnings
 C the calculation of what constitutes a substantial capital sum

3 'In practice you would require more than **this** ...' (line 28)
 A £26,000   B £650,000   C £5,981

4 '... but remember that **that** is exactly what you, and everyone else will effectively be doing in your retirement.' (line 70)
 A living off pension   C living off investments
 B living off the state

Language focus

1 Match these words and phrases with their meanings.

1	FTSE100 index	A	shares in the ownership of a company
2	yield	B	the amount produced from an investment
3	cash buffer	C	the level of interest paid on a cash investment
4	earnings	D	an amount of money held above the minimum level required to counter any risk
5	stocks	E	a tax reduction to promote a specific commercial activity or investment
6	cash deposit rate	F	another term for salary/wages
7	tax break	G	an amount of money available
8	capital sum	H	short for Financial Times Stock Exchange Index – an index of share prices often used as a measure of business prosperity

2 Write the adjectives in bold from the text next to their synonyms.

A **bumper** year for share dividends lies ahead, despite a **looming** recession.

Then you need a **substantial** capital sum.

… you would need a cash buffer to smooth over ~~irregular~~ dividend payments.

… international **high-yielding** stocks with **strong** balance sheets …

… stocks with more **modest** yields but good prospects of **rapid** dividend growth.

1 uneven/variable ...._irregular_.........
2 stable/secure ....
3 significant/large ....
4 quick/fast ....
5 exceptional/bountiful ....
6 profitable/lucrative ....
7 moderate/unexceptional ....
8 imminent/impending ....

3 Complete the sentences with the correct word.

1 We've made a good investment and we're watching the money roll .._in_.. .
2 Since my husband was made redundant, we've had to get .... on my earnings alone.
3 There are good prospects .... making money with this investment.
4 Since we retired, we've been living .... our investments.
5 The amount of dividends paid out is reliant ...... how much profit is made.

Review

Imagine that you are a small business owner and you want to put €50,000 of the company's profit into an investment plan. Go online and read the money sections of several business media websites. Where would you choose to invest the money and why?

18 Watching the markets

Getting started

It's Tuesday 7 February and you are watching the markets online. Read the Market Snapshot of what happened yesterday in the US stock exchange. Remember that you are looking at the graphs in real time because the markets are open at the moment.

Read the headline and the first paragraph carefully, then scan over the rest of the article below in just 30 seconds and answer this question. Have most shares fallen or risen today?

US stocks drop as Greece struggles for accord

S&P 500, Nasdaq Composite break winning streaks

By Kate Gibson, MarketWatch

NEW YORK (MarketWatch) — US stocks retreated from multi-year highs Monday as Greece struggled for an agreement on spending cuts needed to ensure another round of rescue funds.

'This week the focus is on central banks, with the Bank of England meeting and the European Central Bank talking about their monetary policy. There's not a ton of market-moving data for the US, so that along with Greece, is going to keep us focused on things overseas,' said Paul Nolte, managing director at Dearborn Partners in Chicago.

Losing ground after finishing Friday at its highest level since May 2008, the Dow Jones Industrial Average on Monday shed 17.10 points, or 0.1%, to 12,845.13.

19 of the Dow's 30 components slid, with Boeing Co. among the decliners, down 1.15%, after the plane manufacturer said work had begun to repair a fault in its 787 Dreamliner.

Bank of America Corp., the index's best performer year to date, gained 1.7% Monday, leading Dow advancers.

The S&P 500 shed 0.57 point, or 0.04%, at 1,344.33, its first down day in four. As of Friday, the S&P 500 had made its strongest start of the year since 1987, gaining 6.9%.

Financials and materials were the worst performing and energy the best of its 10 industry groups.

Investors are rotating out of utilities, consumer staples and other defensive sectors and buying into those viewed as more risky, noted Nolte.

The Nasdaq Composite declined 3.67 points, or 0.1%, to 2,901.99, its first down day in five and coming off a December 2000 high reached Friday.

For every two stocks rising, three fell on the New York Stock Exchange, where 687 million shares traded. NYSE composite volume was 3.3 billion.

Commodities fell along with equities, with crude futures down 93 cents to settle at $96.91 a barrel and gold futures down $15.40 to close at $1,724.90 an ounce.

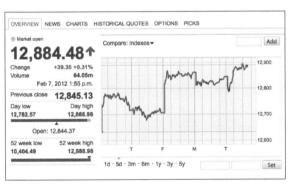

Dow Jones Industrial Average

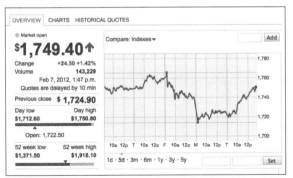

Dow Jones Industrial AverageGold – Electronic (Comex) Feb 2012

Understanding

Fill the blanks in the table below to show how the three main US stock market indexes performed today, then answer the question that follows.

Index	Lost / gained in points	Lost / gained in percentage	Closing figure
Dow Jones Industrial Average	−17.10		
S&P 500			
Nasdaq Composite			

The businesses on which index saw the smallest fall in share prices?

....

Developing your reading skills

1 You have interests in the following markets. Scan over the text and note down how they performed today.

1 Boeing Co.   −1.15%

2 Bank of America Corp.   ....

3 Crude oil   ....

4 Gold   ....

2 Read the graphs intensively to answer these questions.

1 How many days do the graphs show data for?

....

2 What level is the Dow Jones Industrial Average (DJIA) at the moment in real time?

....

3 Has the DJIA fallen or risen since markets opened this morning? By how much?

....

4 What is the lowest point that the DJIA has reached over the last 52 weeks?

....

5 On which day did the DJIA reach its highest point?

....

6 What was the price of gold at the previous close of markets?

....

7 On which day did gold hit its lowest price?

....

8 What is the lowest price that gold has reached today?

....

Language focus

1 Match these market terms and sectors with their meanings.

1 commodities

2 equities

3 financials

4 materials

5 utilities

6 consumer staples

7 crude futures

8 gold futures

A another term for stocks or shares

B agreements to buy and sell gold at a fixed price at a particular point in the future

C organizations that discover, develop, and process raw materials, for example metals, chemicals or forestry products

D basic goods that can be traded on the financial markets

E organizations that make and sell basic consumer products, for example, food, drink, tobacco, prescription drugs and household products

F organizations that deal with money, for example, banks and building societies

G organizations that supply a public service, for example electricity, water or public transport

H agreements to buy and sell oil at a fixed price at a particular point in the future

2 The words in the box below are related to market trends. Write them under the correct heading.

advance	decline	fell	gain	retreated	rise	shed	slid

To describe shares going up in value	To describe shares going down in value
advance	

3 Complete the sentences with the correct preposition(s).

1 The FTSE is ...*at*... its highest level since June.

2 Gold futures made their strongest start to the year .... 2007.

3 Kays Manufacturing has had its first down day .... five.

4 Investors are prone .... knee-jerk reactions when times get bad.

5 This week the focus is .... commodities.

6 Crude futures fell .... 56 cents to settle .... $94.51.

7 Hays Pharmaceuticals has been the index's strongest performer year .... date.

8 For every share rising .... the London Stock Exchange, three shares fell.

Review

Imagine that you have $100,000 to invest. Set up an imaginary portfolio of shares across a variety of companies. Read the market reviews every day for a week to see how your investments perform. At the end of the week, work out how much money you have made/lost.

Reading business blogs

Getting started

1   Read <u>just the title</u> of the blog and predict what it is most likely to be about.

    A We can improve our own chances of long-term success by learning from Japanese business customs.

    B Japanese business customs can teach us how to live for longer.

    C Japanese culture and heritage is key to why they are so successful in business today.

2   Now skim through the blog in just 30 seconds, check your answer to 1, and answer this question: What type of blog is it?

    A Personal business blog

    B Media business blog

    C Corporate blog

Home > Insights > Heritage, Culture and What the Japanese Can Teach Us About Business Longevity

search our site

Heritage, Culture and What the Japanese Can Teach Us About Business Longevity

By Danny Brown

If you take a look at a list of the oldest companies in the world, you'll see the glaringly obvious fact that the majority of the companies listed are Japanese. So why does Japan have such a strong command of business, and what it takes to survive?

There are a few reasons. As someone who's heavily influenced by Japanese culture, one of the things I've always admired about their business approach is how they encourage innovation and information-sharing from the bottom up. Everyone has a voice – it may not be used, but it *will* be heard.

Another reason is the permanent employment system Japanese companies use. This sees workers employed from college, but without a particular skill set to take to their new job. So, instead of being stuck in one division, the new recruit really does learn all about the company and its culture as he or she works their way through it.

Yet perhaps the biggest pointer on why Japanese companies often succeed where others fail is due to one simple reason, and one that's more prevalent through smaller companies as opposed to the larger ones.

New employees are given mentors, and they spend years learning their craft, honing their skills and understanding every part of a machination or process that their employer goes through every day. They focus on needs and future needs as opposed to current successes.

So, simply put, knowing what you're talking about and how to transfer that to what your customer needs is the secret of not only Japanese business' longevity, but longevity in general when it comes to you too.

- **Make your blog** your fountain of knowledge as opposed to your drainpipe of loose facts.

- **Make your speeches** your topic of personal knowledge as opposed to an Internet-searched equivalent.

- **Make your business** the one that finds the answers it doesn't have, as opposed to your customers finding them first elsewhere.

- **Make your job** the one that educates you for your next position as opposed to the one that educates you on killing time.

- **Make the books** you read enhance your knowledge as opposed to entrench your growth

We all want long-term success. We all want to be recognized or known for what we do, long after we don't do it anymore. But sometimes we think achieving longevity is something others do, not us.

The funny thing is, longevity is a lot easier to come by than we think it is – you just have to know how to find it, and funnel it.

Ready to start learning?

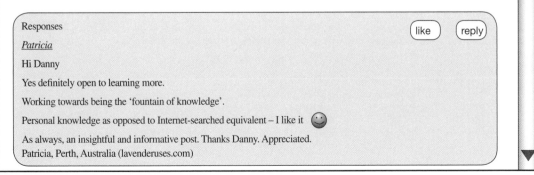

Responses   (like) (reply)

Patricia

Hi Danny

Yes definitely open to learning more.

Working towards being the 'fountain of knowledge'.

Personal knowledge as opposed to Internet-searched equivalent – I like it 🙂

As always, an insightful and informative post. Thanks Danny. Appreciated.

Patricia, Perth, Australia (lavenderuses.com)

Adapted from http://dannybrown.me/2012/01/11/japanese-business-success/

Understanding

Are the following statements True or False? Correct any that are false.

1 Most of the world's longest surviving companies are Japanese.

....

2 Japanese companies do not welcome suggestions from employees in junior ranks.

....

3 Employees in Japan tend to stay with one company and work their way up.

....

4 The mentoring system encourages Japanese businesses to focus on current successes.

....

5 The blogger recommends that people make speeches based on Internet research.

....

6 Patricia's comment suggests that she disagrees with the main points in the blog.

....

Developing your reading skills

1 **The blogger uses signposting language to link phrases and sentences together. Identify why he uses the words in bold, by matching them to the explanations and synonyms below.**

1 **Another reason is** the permanent employment system Japanese companies use.

E............

2 ... workers employed from college, but without a particular skill set to take to their new job. **So,** instead of being stuck in one division, the new recruit really does learn all about the company ...

....

3 **Yet** perhaps the biggest pointer on why Japanese companies often succeed where others fail is due to one simple reason ... /**But** sometimes we think achieving longevity is something others do, not us.

....

4 So, **simply put**, knowing what you're talking about and how to transfer that to what your customer needs ...

....

5 They focus on needs and future needs **as opposed to** current successes.

....

A To clarify a point (synonym: in other words, basically).

B To provide contrast/balance (synonym: however, besides).

C To show consequence (synonym: therefore, consequently).

D To contrast two different points (synonym: instead of, in the place of).

E ~~To make an additional point (synonym: in addition, what is more).~~

2 Do you agree with the points that Danny made in his blog? Why/Why not? Write a brief comment to post at the end of his blog expressing your opinion on the subject.

....

....

....

Language focus

1 Match these blogging terms with their meanings.

1 blogger   **A** receive or obtain a blog regularly via RSS feed

2 response   **B** web feed format that shows when new content has been added to blogs

3 subscribe to a blog

     C software required to view RSS data

4 blogosphere   **D** person who writes the blog

5 RSS   **E** place where you can write a comment about the blog

6 feed reader   **F** the blogging community as a whole

2 Rewrite these sentences, replacing the underlined sections with one of the phrases from the box.

be heavily influenced by	hone your skills
have a strong command of	be a fountain of knowledge
~~particular skill set~~	

1 We had several applicants with no <u>specialized area of ability</u>.
We had several applicants with no particular skill set.....................................

2 A Personal Assistant must <u>be very good at</u> multi-tasking.

....

3 Our work ethic here <u>is affected greatly by</u> our Australian partners.

....

4 He <u>is very knowledgeable</u> when it comes to blogging.

....

5 You should take this opportunity to <u>perfect your technique</u>.

....

Review

Go to a blog search engine and find a blog that is relevant to your line of work. Use the skills that you have practised in this unit to read it. Then comment on it to share your opinions about the piece.

20 Reading business books

Getting started

Skim over the extract from the business book *The Leadership Engine* by Noel M. Tichy in just two minutes. Which of these business book categories does this book fall into?

1 Careers advice books, giving you tips on how to advance professionally.

2 How-to books, showing you the methods required to perform certain business functions that you may not be familiar with.

3 Reference books that give you information on a particular area of business.

4 Books that suggest effective business styles and strategies that can help you improve the way you work.

5 Books about personal finance.

6 Business biographies and autobiographies.

Winning Organizations are Teaching Organizations

Why do some companies succeed while others fail?

The answer that I have come up with is that winning companies win because they have good leaders who nurture the development of other leaders at all levels of the organization. The ultimate test of success for an organization is not whether it can win today but whether it can keep winning tomorrow and the day after. Therefore, the ultimate test for a leader is not whether he or she makes smart decisions and takes decisive action, but whether he or she teaches the others to be leaders and builds an organization that can sustain its success even when he or she is not around. The key ability of winning organizations and winning leaders is creating leaders. ...

... The winning organizations and people who do this well come in all shapes, sizes, and nationalities, and can be found in any industry. The goods and services they produce and the strategies and tactics they employ are widely divergent. But they all share a set of fundamentals.

- First, leaders with a proven track record of success take direct responsibility for the development of other leaders.

- Second, leaders who develop other leaders have teachable points of view in the specific areas of ideas, values, and something that I call E-cubed – emotional energy and edge. Winning leaders/teachers have ideas that they can articulate and teach to others about both how to make the organization successful in the marketplace and how to develop other leaders. They have teachable values about the kinds of behavior that will lead to organizational and personal success. They deliberately generate positive emotional energy in others. And they demonstrate and encourage others to demonstrate edge, which is the ability to face reality and make tough decisions.

- Third, leaders embody their teachable points of view in living stories. They tell stories about their pasts that explain their learning experiences and their beliefs. And they create stories about the future of their organizations that engage others, both emotionally and intellectually, to attain the winning future that they describe.

- Finally, because winning leaders invest considerable time developing other leaders, they have well-defined methodologies and coaching and teaching techniques. Among these is the willingness to admit mistakes and show their vulnerabilities in order to serve as effective role models for others. ...

... This is a book about winners. Who are they? What separates them from the losers? And what can you do to make sure that you and your organization are winners as well? ...

... The companies that win will be those that build and maintain a steady focus on developing leaders at all levels of the company. ...

Adapted from *The Leadership Engine*, Noel M. Tichy.

Understanding

Answer the following questions.

1 How does Tichy define a winning company?

   ....

2 What does Tichy think is the most important role of a leader?

   ....

3 What are the three key areas that Tichy wants leaders to teach to others?

   ....

4 How does Tichy believe leaders should draw on their past in their teaching?

   ....

5 Does Tichy ever believe leaders should show a vulnerable side. Why/why not?

   ....

Developing your reading skills

1 **Work out the most likely meanings of the words in bold from the context without using a dictionary.**

1 The goods and services they produce and the strategies and tactics they employ are widely **divergent**. But they all share a set of fundamentals.

   A similar to each other   **B** different to each other   **C** the same as each other

2 And they demonstrate and encourage others to demonstrate **edge**, which is the ability to face reality and make tough decisions.

   A moving slowly towards something   **C** force, effectiveness

   B the thin sharp side of something

3 Third, leaders **embody** their teachable points of view in living stories.

   A represent   **B** tell stories about   **C** teach

2 **When you read a business book, it is useful to determine the author's point of view. Do you think that Noel M. Tichy would agree or disagree with the following speakers?**

1 'We send our managers on external training courses because we senior managers simply don't have the time to spend training them ourselves.'

   Agree   ⟨Disagree⟩

2 'Leaders need to know effective methods for teaching others.'

   Agree   Disagree

3 'The most important quality in a leader is to make difficult decisions and follow through with appropriate action.'

   Agree   Disagree

4 'We must put in place strategies that will ensure the continued success of our business in the future by developing the leaders who will take our places.'

   Agree   Disagree

5 'I'm not a teacher, I'm a businessperson. It's not my job to train others.'

   Agree   Disagree

Language focus

1 Write the verbs in bold next to their meanings below.

'Winning leaders/teachers have ideas that they can **articulate** and teach to others about both how to make the organization successful in the marketplace and how to **develop** other leaders'

'They deliberately **generate** positive emotional energy in others. And they **demonstrate** and ~~encourage~~ others to demonstrate edge,'

1 give somebody support and confidence   *encourage*
2 create by training and teaching   ....
3 show that you have a skill or quality   ....
4 express your ideas clearly in words   ....
5 cause something to begin   ....

2 Complete the sentences with the correct preposition.

1 The ultimate test *of* success for a business is how they train their leaders.
2 The key ability .... successful leaders is generating positive emotional energy in others.
3 If you have a proven track record .... success, then you must consider how to carry that forward into the future.
4 Managers need to take direct responsibility .... training the employees who work for them.
5 The CEO of a business needs to serve .... a role model for all employees.
6 Let's maintain a steady focus .... our objectives for the day.

3 Insert the missing words into the text below.

smart	behavior	behaviour	clever

You can tell that *The Leadership Engine* has been written by an American author because:

• use of American vocabulary rather than British vocabulary, for example '.................' instead of '.................'.
• use of American spelling, for example, '.................' rather than '.........................'.

Review

How far do you agree with Noel M. Tichy's argument? Why/Why not?

....

....

....

ANSWER KEY

Unit 1

Getting started

1

1 He should read Nora Stephens' email first because it is marked as 'urgent' and the word 'urgently' was used in the subject field.
2 Pierre Valois – he attached sales reports.
3 Li Sung – she sent the programme for the upcoming conference.

2

Email 1 does not ask him to take any further action and is for reference only, so he could leave it until later to read in detail.

Understanding

1

Email 1: Li Sung   Email 3: Nora Stephens
Email 2: Pierre Valois

2

1 False – all senior management are expected to attend the conference.
2 True
3 False – there was a delay in sending the sales reports to Alex.
4 False – there are some unresolved issues regarding January's figures.
5 False – Alex must approve the budgets by 2 p.m. today.
6 True

Developing your reading skills

1

	Email 1	Email 2	Email 3
To send Alex information about something	✓	✓	
To ask Alex to do something		✓	✓
To apologize about a delay in something	✓	✓	
To invite a response from Alex regarding something		✓	✓

2

Email 1 B Not urgent, look at when time allows.
Email 2 C Look at first thing tomorrow to sort out unresolved issue.
Email 3 A Approve budgets right away.

Language focus

1

1 sender, recipient
2 subject
3 attachment
4 cc, bcc
5 reply, reply all

2

Purpose	More formal expression	Less formal expression
To start an email	Dear Alex,	Hi Alex,
To advise about information sent with email	Please find below …	The sales reports are attached.
To ask somebody to do something	I would appreciate it if you could …	Could you possibly … ?
To apologize about something	I apologize for …	Sorry for …
To invite a response from the recipient	I look forward to your reply.	Look forward to hearing from you.
To end an email/express gratitude	Thank you in advance,	Thanks,

3

1 close of play
2 in the loop
3 some loose ends to tie up
4 in due course
5 give somebody the green light on something

Unit 2

Getting started

The best summary of the situation is:

3 There is a problem with the Traverse software, which manages the company's travel arrangements, that is unresolved.

Understanding

1 Because there is a problem [a glitch] in the Traverse computer systems. ('Because they have paid double commission to some external travel agencies' is also possible.)

2 Yes, there were similar problems last year.

3 She brings in Tom Becaveric to get his opinion on the situation

4 $150,000

5 Tom brings in Xavier Justino to get information from him and Dina Finn to fix a meeting.

6 Tom has called a meeting with all interested parties to try to resolve the problem.

Developing your reading skills

1

This is the best response from Xavier:

1 I'm afraid that this is the first I've heard about this problem, but I'll get my team onto it straight away and update you at the meeting tomorrow.

2

1 Xavier B Find out exactly what went wrong with the Traverse system in time for tomorrow's meeting so that I can explain it to my colleagues.

2 Ben E/F Find out how many agencies we've overpaid and let everybody concerned know the exact cost/ Email the affected travel agencies to inform them of the technical error.

3 Dina A Set up a meeting for tomorrow morning and send out an email to invite the attendees.

4 Jacky D Get Ben to find out exactly how much money we have overpaid.

5 Xavier, Tom, Ben, and Jacky C Prepare for and attend the meeting tomorrow at 9.30 a.m.

3

1 Tom Becaveric
2 Xavier Justino
3 Jacky Miller
4 Ben Wade

Language focus

1

Phrases requesting further information	Phrases promising further information
Any thoughts? Please advise ASAP. What are your thoughts on this?	I'll get back to you as soon as I can. Ben will circulate exact figures shortly. We will keep you updated.

2

1 get
2 glitch
3 bottom
4 attention
5 present

Review

(Answers will vary. Suggested answer only.)

There's been another problem with the Traverse software and there's going to be a meeting to find out what went wrong and sort the problem out.

Unit 3

Getting started

3 Li Sung is writing to Nicola Mann to complain about a number of factors regarding her company's conference held at Grants Hotel on 23 April.

Understanding

1

1 Equipment: projectors for presenting material from laptops were unavailable. They had to get one sent from their office at their own expense.

2 Facilities: conference room was overheated; material from the previous day's conference was lying around; not enough tables and chairs were supplied.

3 Catering: service was delayed and food was mediocre and lukewarm.

2

1

1 The hotel has three projectors but all were out of order due to circumstances beyond their control.

2 Due to an error in internal checks.

3 Due to unusually high number of kitchen staff off sick.

2

1 It was an isolated incident and they'll make sure it doesn't happen again. They'll reimburse the cost of transporting projector.

2 They have implemented a new checking system.

3 They have changed their staffing rota to ensure that they always have sufficient cover should situation reoccur. They have offered a 10 per cent discount on their next booking with the hotel.

Developing your reading skills

1

(Answers will vary. Suggested answers only.)

1 I've had a complaint from Li Sung regarding the fact that we didn't have any projectors available for her conference. Please advise ASAP on how this was allowed to happen.

2 I've had a complaint from Li Sung regarding the facilities for her conference – the conference room was overheated and untidy and there weren't enough tables and chairs set up. What are your thoughts on this?

3 I've had a complaint from Li Sung about the catering for her conference – she said the service was delayed and the food was mediocre and lukewarm. Any thoughts?

2

1 B It was Jason Philips' fault that we didn't have a projector.

2 B I expect a reply to this email soon.

3 A It wasn't our fault.

4 B We didn't check the room properly.

5 A I'm about to offer you some form of compensation, even though we're not legally obliged to ...

Language focus

2

A To apologize	B To explain the reasons for the problems
Please accept our sincere apologies for … I regret that we fell short of your requirements. There is really no excuse for it and I apologize for this.	The problem arose because of… Unfortunately the problems that day resulted from… …due to circumstances beyond our control.
C To provide reassurance that the problems will not happen again	**D To offer compensation**
…to ensure that such problems do not reoccur. I'll personally ensure that this never happens again. Please rest assured that this was an isolated incident, which we'll ensure never reoccurs.	As a gesture of goodwill, I propose that we… Additionally, we can offer…

Review

(Answers will vary. Suggested answer only.)
Nicola Mann responded well to my complaint and has offered us a 10 per cent discount for future bookings.

Unit 4

Getting started

1 B Ayisha Khabbazeh – Manufacturing

2 C Nicola Mann – Hotel management

3 A Charlotte Ring – Interior design

4 D Peter Harrop – Photography

Understanding

1 False – Ayisha Khabbazeh works for a company that has offices in Shanghai and London/Charlotte Ring works for a company that has an office in New York.

2 True

3 False – Patrick Brook is PA to Ayisha Khabbazeh.

4 False – they all have PAs, but some of them share them.

5 False – Ayisha Khabbazeh has been at Fordhams since 2000.

6 False – as Vice-President, she oversaw the daily operations of the company and developed strategic customer relationships.

Developing your reading skills

1

1 No, but I've got his website address, so you could try that – www.peterharrop.com

2 Yes, it's ringsdesignservices@contact.com

3 Yes, one in London and one in Shanghai.

4 Yes, it's Nicola Mann on 207 2839 2839.

2

1 Kitty Waters, PA to R&D Director

2 Somebody in the HR department – Lin Yao or Isla Horley.

3 Somebody in the Finance department – Jessica Millwood or Imogen Clark.

4 Ayisha Khabbazeh

5 Somebody in the Sales & Marketing department – Matine Raza or Dina Finn

6 Tamsin Cox, PA to Ku Ming

Language focus

1

Work in a more senior position to somebody	Work at the same level as somebody	Work for somebody
manage oversee supervise	collaborate with work with	be a direct report of be managed by report to/into

2

1 oversees/manages/supervises
2 is colleagues with/collaborates with/works with
3 is a direct report of/is managed by/reports to/into
4 oversees/manages/supervises
5 is a direct report of/is managed by/reports to/into
6 is colleagues with/collaborates with/works with
7 oversees/manages/supervises
8 is a direct report of/is managed by/reports to/into
9 is colleagues with/collaborates with/works with

Review

(Answers will vary. Suggested answers only.)
I'm a Sales & Marketing Director.
I manage the Sales & Marketing Manager and oversee the work of the whole department.
I work with the other directors – the HR Director, the Finance Director, the Manufacturing Director and the R&D Director.
I report into the Vice-President.

Unit 5

Getting started

April
17 April   Client meeting to discuss amendments to draft one designs.
30 April   Revised designs to our team for cost assessment

May
7 May   Cost assessment submitted to me and CEO
31 May   Approval date of new costings and design revisions

Understanding

1   7 May
2   31 May
3   15 June
4   $0.6 million
5   $1.6 million
6   $3 million

Developing your reading skills

1

17 April	Meeting with our design and commercial team to discuss amendments to the draft designs.
20 April	Delivery of draft contract to you
14 May	Feedback on draft contract to our legal team
20 May	Revised contract sent to you
31 May	All contractual details finalized
1 June	Final designs submitted to you
15 June	Final designs approved by you Final contracts signed

2

Budget area	Hill View original budget	Meridian Way additional costs	Updated Hill View budget
1 Design and architectural	$0.9 million	$0.3 million	$1.2 million
2 Site clearance	$0.4 million	$0.1 million	$0.5 million
3 Mechanical/ engineering	$5.8 million	$0.7 million	$6.5 million
4 Labour hire	$0.9 million	$0.1 million	$1 million

New forecast profit is $1.8 million

Language focus

1   E send something to somebody for consideration
2   F allocate a task to somebody
3   B formally give your consent to something
4   G write your signature
5   D finish something
6   C make something final
7   A prepare a new edited version of something

(Answers will vary. Suggested answer only.)

Dear Jo,

The schedule dates all look fine and have been approved by the client.

However, we will need to amend the budget because I received some late costs from the Meridian Way project on which it was based. The following sections will need to be revised:

	Existing budget	Revised figures
Design/architectural:	$0.9 million	$1.2 million
Site clearance:	$0.4 million	$0.5 million
Mechanical/engineering	$5.8 million	$6.5 million
Labour hire:	$0.9 million	$1 million

I'll make the necessary revisions and forward the budget to the CEO and FD for review.

Best regards,
James

Unit 6

Getting started

1 ✓   3 ✓   5 ✗
2 ✗   4 ✗   6 ✓

Understanding

1 10.30 in Meeting room 6
2 Sara Filfil was the chair and Rory Morgan took minutes.
3 He noted that the order had not yet been placed for the new SJE12 sales software, which was approved at the last meeting.
4 Down by 2.4%
5 Nobody
6 Hannah Pepper

Developing your reading skills

1

Attendee	Action point	Deadline
Sara Filfil	To purchase SJE12 sales software	By next meeting
Adam Lamb	To research upcoming promotions by major competitors	For presentation at next meeting
Tanya Prakash	To circulate sample version of new quarterly newsletter	By 15 April
All attendees	To provide feedback on newsletter to Tanya Prakash	By end of April
Hannah Pepper	To coordinate collection for HR Director's maternity present	By 8 April

2

1 Accurate
2 Accurate
3 Inaccurate – minutes state sales results down by 2.4%
4 Accurate
5 Inaccurate – minutes state Hannah Pepper exceeded her target by 8%
6 Inaccurate – minutes state that Hannah Pepper made this proposal.

Language focus

1

1 C the place where the meeting takes place
2 H arranged by someone for a particular time
3 A the person who controls the meeting, ensuring that it runs to time and that all points of the agenda are covered
4 B a person who is present at the meeting
5 E the person who takes notes during the meeting and will write up and distribute the minutes of the meeting
6 F a message sent to a meeting to advise that one of the attendees will be unable to attend
7 I the point in the meeting when those present at the last meeting must state that they are happy with the minutes from that meeting
8 J issues for discussion
9 D short for 'Any Other Business': the point at which people can raise other issues that are not on the agenda
10 G short for 'not applicable': this explains a lack of information in a field or on a form because it is not relevant to the situation

2

1 Kay Peterson to <u>circulate</u> annual report to all board members.
2 Nicky Chisholm to <u>research</u> ways of reducing overheads.
3 Roz Toole to <u>purchase</u> new photocopier for department.
4 Sophie Jesman to <u>coordinate</u> a meeting with all department heads.
5 Liam Chu to <u>provide feedback on</u> presentations at company conference.

Review

(Answers will vary. Suggested answer only.)
The main points were that March sales were down 2.4% from last month, but we all still met our sales targets. We think the drop in sales was due to the promotion run by Mastersons this month. There are two new incentives: first, if we exceed our sales targets by more than 15%, we will receive an increased commission of 7.5% and second, in December, they are going to give a five-star holiday for a family of four to the highest seller in the whole company.

Unit 7

Getting started

(Suggested answers only)
1   Yes, it is worth looking at the CV because this applicant's covering letter is well-crafted and shows that he fits many of the criteria required by the job.
2   Yes, it is worth taking the time to read this CV in detail because the applicant seems to have lots of relevant experience and qualifications.

Understanding

1   False – Stephen Nicholas is a fully qualified accountant with 12 years' post-qualification experience.
2   True
3   False – he is looking for a new job because his company has recently relocated to Kent and he is looking for a job nearer home.
4   False – he has no direct experience in the food industry.
5   True
6   False – he worked in Cyprus from June 2002 to October 2005.

Developing your reading skills

1

[5]   A A concluding line to draw attention to the CV that is enclosed with your letter (or attached with your email).
[3]   B A paragraph to show how your experience and personal skills tie in with the job requirements.
[1]   C A reference line to summarize for the recipient what your letter is about.
[4]   D An explanation of why you are looking for a new position.
[2]   E An introductory paragraph explaining what position you are applying for and where you saw it advertised.

2

- qualified accountant + five years of experience ✓
- experience of managing a team ✓
- knowledge of UKGAAP and IFRS ✓
- excellent Excel skills ✓
- ability to multi-task ✓
- attention to detail
- ability to work under pressure to tight deadlines ✓
- good communication skills

Language focus

1

Definition	CV word/phrase
a term to describe your employment history to date	work experience
a person who knows you well and is prepared to write a letter on your behalf about your character and abilities	referee
the knowledge and ability to do something well	skill
examinations that you have passed	qualifications
the things that you enjoy doing	interests
the ability to carry out a task or job	competency
something that you are required to do as part of your job	responsibility

2

1   C made changes in order to improve
2   E took part in
3   D organized
4   B handed over formally
5   A communicated and stayed in contact with

3

1   of
2   for
3   under
4   of
5   to

Review

(Answers will vary. Suggested answer only)
A fully-qualified accountant with 12 years post-qualification experience, Stephen is currently a Senior Finance Manager at Desmarais UK, overseeing a finance department of 12 accountants. He says that he can work under pressure to tight deadlines and is able to multi-task. I think he's a good candidate because he has all the qualifications and competencies required and a number of the qualities that we're looking for too.

Unit 8

Getting started

2 A Financial Controller at a leading engineering company.

Understanding

1 Bespoke engineering components

2 He or she is in charge of the day-to-day financial activities of the company.

3 He or she must be a qualified accountant.

4 Experience of managing a team.

5 A self-starter and able to work under pressure.

Developing your reading skills

1

1 ✓	3 ✗	5 ✗
2 ✗	4 ✓	6 ✓

2

Extract from appraisal form	Requirement as set out in job description	Rating
1 I have put in place a two-year plan to reduce operating costs by 10%.	• Developing strategies to ensure effective management of company's finances.	2
2 I have produced the financial pack on time every month and circulated it to all directors.	• Preparing monthly financial reporting pack for the Board of Directors.	2
3 I have managed the Finance team of 12 effectively, and have successfully recruited two new employees.	• Managing a team of 12 accountants.	1
4 I have overseen the production of statutory accounts that were satisfactory both internally and externally.	• Drafting statutory accounts for company that comply with all relevant accounting standards.	2
5 I worked with the auditors to answer queries relating to my department. Also, I dealt with questions relating to Accounts Receivable department because manager was on leave during the audit.	• Liaising with external auditors and supplying them with all relevant information.	1
6 There were some issues with the internal accounting system, which I should have addressed earlier. These have now been resolved and one of my objectives is to ensure that such problems do not reoccur.	• Overseeing the internal accounting system to ensure effective management of accounts.	3

Language focus

1 communication skills

2 proven track record

3 proactive self-starter

4 energy and drive

5 multi-task

6 under pressure

7 team player

8 attention to detail

Review

Answers will vary. See covering letter on page 28 in Unit 7 as a model answer.

Unit 9

Getting started

In order to:	Report section
• read the main part of the report detailing the information that has been discovered.	Main findings
• know why the report was commissioned.	Introduction
• read a short summary of the 'Main Findings' section.	Conclusions
• focus on suggestions of how any issues or problems could be dealt with.	Recommendations
• read a summary of all the key points in each section of report.	Executive summary
• find out exactly what appears on each page of the report.	Contents
• know about methods that were used to carry out the research contained in the report.	Procedure
• know if there is any additional relevant information, which is not directly related to the subject of the report.	Appendices

Understanding

1 B 18%
2 C previous customers and existing customers
3 B Because check-in time requirements have increased.
4 A They should do more marketing on the Internet and improve their website.
5 C They should revert to the old check-in time requirements for premium seats and approach financial institutions directly.

Developing your reading skills

1

1 C	3 D	5 E
2 A	4 B	

2

1 Task 2A
2 Task 1C
3 Task 5E
4 Task 4B
5 Task 3D

Language focus

1

1 D try to find out more about
2 B think about carefully
3 E sort out a disagreement
4 G raise your profile/be more active in
5 H spend money on
6 A offer for sale
7 C gradually make better and stronger
8 F discuss

2

1 by
2 on
3 of, of/into, of/into
4 amongst/among/on
5 of, for

Review

(Answers will vary. Suggested answer only)
Yes, I have. The main recommendations of the report were that we need to:
• investigate and change new premium seat check-in times.
• resolve the dispute with cabin crew.
• offer more cut-price tickets.
• increase our Internet presence and improve the website.
• target large financial institutions to market premium fares.

Unit 10

Getting started

Yes, they have had a good year – they've reported a strong result, which is better than last year, and all the subsidiaries were profitable.

Understanding

1 D Dividend
2 C Investment in people
3 A Financial summary
4 E Outlook
5 B Investment in products and services

Developing your reading skills

1

1	page 16	4	page 20
2	page 14	5	pages 4 and 6
3	page 40	6	page 18

2

1 There was a higher level of cash held in 2007 than in 2011.

2 There was a lower level of revenue in 2009 than in 2011.

3 There was a lower level of operating cash flow in 2009 than in 2011.

4 There was a lower level of profit before tax in 2007 than in 2008.

5 There was a higher level of revenue in 2008 than in 2011.

6 There was a lower level of cash held in 2009 than in 2011.

7 There was a higher level of profit before tax in 2011 than in 2009.

3

(Answers will vary. Suggested answers only.)
Yes, I would consider joining FlySky Airlines because the company looks in good shape. Their annual report shows that all their subsidiaries have been profitable this year, and there has been increased revenue and profit after tax.
No, I wouldn't consider joining FlySky Airlines because, although they have had a good year, their results have fluctuated over the last few years and they warn of challenging times ahead.

Language focus

1

1 B the return made by a business after operating costs have been deducted, but before tax has been charged

2 D the return made by a business after operating costs and tax have been deducted

3 E the amount of money that a business generates from its main activities

4 A the amount of money that a business keeps

5 C the income of a business on its main activities

2

1 yield/return
2 capital
3 dividend
4 capacity
5 margin

3

1 of
2 in, of
3 on
4 to
5 of

Review

(Answers will vary. Suggested answer only.)
FlySky Airlines have had a good year. Their revenue has increased by 6.3% on last year to $8,892 million and their profit after tax has increased by 8.2% on last year to $198 million. All their subsidiaries have been profitable and they've invested in three new Airbus 345s and refitted 24 Boeing 747s. They have appointed a new CEO, Deborah Chirrey, and are paying a dividend of $9.20 per share.

Unit 11

Getting started

Advertisement 3 from Harrison and Evans School of Management may be of interest.

Understanding

1 A A company that recruits senior to mid-level managers.

2 C An IT company that designs or customizes software to meet client requirements.

3 B A company offering management training courses.

4 A A new business magazine.

Developing your reading skills

1

Information	Included	Not included
1 Information about the types of companies that Patel Ballard Executive Recruitment Consultants work with.		

Information	Included	Not included
2 Names of the companies that Patel Ballard Executive Recruitment Consultants work with.		✓
3 A detailed breakdown of all services provided by Simenons Software Solutions.		✓
4 Details about the cost of Harrison and Evans School of Management courses.		✓
5 A detailed breakdown of the types of article that will be appearing in *Strategia*.	✓	
6 A link for readers to get a special discount by subscribing early to *Strategia*.	✓	

2

1 Opinion
2 Information
3 Information
4 Information
5 Opinion
6 Information
7 Opinion
8 Information

Language focus

1

1 D skilful/knowledgeable
2 F thorough/in a lot of detail
3 A concerning or including the whole world
4 C absolutely necessary
5 B useful or worth a lot of money
6 G developed for a particular purpose
7 E of good quality

2

1	in	4	of
2	at	5	to
3	for	6	for

3

1 This new updated software is <u>second to none</u>.
2 We're thinking too much about the detail – we need to <u>look at the big picture</u>.
3 <u>Take my word for it</u> – our product is superior to those of our competitors.
4 Thanks to our new marketing campaign, we have become the <u>first port of call</u> for online computer support.
5 We've <u>got caught up in</u> a legal battle that we didn't want.
6 We're delighted with the new CEO – he seems to <u>be a good fit for our company</u>.

Review

Answers will vary.

Unit 12

Getting started

1

Answers will vary.

2

1 A health insurance company
2 Yes, page 12

Understanding

1 False – Kaymans Inc. offers a range of services: personal health insurance, business health insurance, and travel health insurance. But not car or home insurance.
2 True
3 False – Kaymans Inc. supplies health cover for large and small companies.
4 True
5 True
6 False – psychiatric cover is available as an additional option.

Developing your reading skills

1 It is suitable because it meets your requirements:
   • Suitable for small business: 'Packages available to suit large or small businesses'
   • Flexible with option of dental and optical cover: 'Flexibility to choose a personalized scheme to meet the requirements of your policyholders.'/'you can add dental care, optical care,'

- Long-standing secure healthcare provider: 'Peace of mind that comes from choosing a health insurer with over 50 years of experience.'

2 (Answers will vary depending on how sceptical the reader is being. Suggested answers only.)

1	?	3	?	5	✓
2	?	4	✓	6	✓

Language focus

1

1 C superior/excellent/of a very good standard
2 F able to change and adapt easily to different conditions
3 A made for a particular individual
4 D done without delay
5 E trustworthy/accurate
6 B with the knowledge and ability to do something well

2

1 on
2 for

3 to
4 of
5 of

3

1 healthcare provider
2 sick day
3 policyholder
4 excess
5 flexible cover
6 core package

Review

(Answers will vary. Suggested answer only.)
The Kaymans Inc. core package includes various types of hospital cover, a private ambulance, and access to a 24-hour helpline. You can tailor the package to suit your needs by setting the level of hospital cover provided, including in a members' excess option, and adding in dental, optical and psychiatric cover.

Unit 13

Getting started

5

Understanding

- Customers are given prompt access to the best doctors and best-equipped hospitals.
- Flexible cover allows customers to create bespoke business plans.
- Price guarantee – if customers find comparable cover cheaper elsewhere, they will refund the difference.
- Offers to help keep their customers healthy – half-price gym membership and health screens.
- 25% discount or first three months free if customers register before October 31.

Developing your reading skills

1 Click here to find out more about our business packages.
2 **ABOUT US**
3 Job opportunities
4 Send us an email to customerservices@rsl.com
5 **INDIVIDUAL**
6 Get an online quotation here.

7 Site map
8 🔍

Language focus

1

1	FAQs	6	Job opportunities
2	About us	7	Privacy policy
3	Register	8	Help
4	Contact us	9	Site map
5	Log in	10	Terms of use

2

1 G online quotation here.
2 D adviser on 0938227388.
3 F an email to customers@web.com.
4 C our database of products and services.
5 A community at www.webcommunity.com.
6 B comparable product for less elsewhere and we'll refund the difference.
7 E before October 31 to be eligible for a discount of up to 25%.

Review

Answers will vary.

Unit 14

Getting started
The launch of a new tablet from Swallows Electronics Manufacturer

Understanding
1 False – Swallows are promoting the launch of their new tablet on World Connections, a social networking site.
2 True
3 True
4 True
5 False – Conterifiraldi wants to know where he or she can buy the Swallows Tablet in Italy.
6 False – Gordonowash is unlikely to buy the new Swallows Tablet.

Developing your reading skills

1
1 Like
2 Dislike
3 Like
4 Like
5 Dislike
6 Don't know

2
1 ✓
2 ✓
3 ✓
4 ✗
5 ✓

6 ✗
7 ✓
8 ✗

Language focus

1
1 B leave a message on somebody's homepage
2 C respond publicly to something on a social networking site
3 A show your approval of something on a social networking site
4 D appear in a sequence of messages in chronological order, with the most recent at the top

2
1 to follow them
2 Tweeters/Twitterers/Tweeple
3 Tweets
4 followers
5 to Tweet

3
1 C Two ways of sending somebody a personal message on Twitter. 'DM' is a direct message and will be seen only by the named follower. '@' replies will appear in the person's timeline and can be seen by other users too.
2 A Two ways of reposting (or repeating) something that has already been said by another Twitterer.
3 B Topics that are being discussed by lots of users are said to be 'trending' and a list of current trending topics is visible on your homepage.

Unit 15

Getting started
2 The gulf between rich and poor could be dangerous for capitalist society.

Understanding
1 True
2 False – Nouriel Roubini was nicknamed Doctor Doom because he highlighted the excesses in the financial system before the crash.
3 True
4 False – Lael Brainard believes that the tax system reinforces the gap between the rich and the poor.

5 False – Mr Roubini thinks that there is now rising inequality in China and other emerging economies too.
6 True

Developing your reading skills

1
1 Agree
2 Agree
3 Agree
4 Agree

So, no he is not providing a balanced debate because all the contributors agree with the statement.

2

(Suggested answers)

Contributor	Argument
Nouriel Roubini	Financial and social imbalances could lead to unrest – we should learn lessons from history, e.g. the boom of the 1920s, followed by the Great Depression led to World War Two.
Lael Brainard	Too much money has been going to the richest in society and the tax system has helped to reinforce this – we need to change this.
Angel Gurría	Unfairly high salaries and greed caused the first financial crisis and it's happening again.
Anders Borg	Companies should behave more morally, investing profits in society to create jobs rather than putting it in tax havens.

Language focus

1

Words related to economic 'good times'	Words related to economic 'bad times'
wealth	austerity measures
gilded age	crash
profits	financial crisis
rewards	losses
	recession
	sovereign debt problems

2

1   B make something less certain or secure
2   E move freely
3   F set off/cause something to happen
4   C draw attention to something
5   A alleviate/lessen the pain of something
6   D make something stronger/boost

3

1   on/about   5   about
2   for   6   in
3   at/towards   7   for
4   to   8   in

4

1   disproportionate
2   excessive
3   rising
4   emerging

Review

(Answers will vary. Suggested answers only.)
Yes, I agree. It is the responsibility of large successful businesses to invest back in society. It makes sense morally to help people who are less fortunate than yourself, and it makes sense financially because investing money in jobs will help to get our economies out of recession and ultimately help our businesses prosper in the future.

No, I disagree. Capitalism is driven by the pursuit of wealth. We try to pursue wealth morally in our business, but if we reinvest all our profits back into society, then we are no longer a capitalist society at all. And businesspeople will see no benefit in working hard to succeed if the rewards are not sufficient.

Unit 16

Getting started

2

1   US bank pushes for Vietnam infrastructure deals
2   Top ten tips for doing business in East Asia

Understanding

1   1 Business / 2 Economy / 3 Markets / 4 Investments / 5 Money
2   Gold falls on yen strength, lower stocks
3   Girling Hamilton and J Regan Motors in $8 billion merger
4   1 Dow Jones / 2 FTSE / 3 Nikkei 225
5   C The latest news about the markets and major businesses

Developing your reading skills

1

1   More markets and currency rates
2   Money/Money guide
3   Euro set to drop further against dollar
4   See all (in Breaking news box)

5   CEO of top bank to waive bonus

6   Girling Hamilton and J Regan Motors in $8 billion merger

7   Work for us

8   Mixed day for profit announcements

2

1   It's 8,459.

2   Yes, Swallows International shares have taken a hit following technical problems.

3   Yes, Haymans and Sons are going to float their shares in September.

4   The euro is set to drop further against the dollar.

5   The FTSE has gone down by 12.40 to 5,229.

6   Gold has fallen because of the strength of the yen.

7   Shares in Sharmans Investment Bank have tumbled by 12% following reports that their profits were down by 48%.

Language focus

1

1   E the very latest stories that have just been published online

2   G in-depth articles and stories

3   F a list of webpages that have been read the most often

4   B a list of webpages that have been recommended the most often by readers to other contacts by way of social media

5   A a data format that enables you to see when a website has added new content, giving you access to all the latest headlines without having to visit each individual webpage

6   C a digital audio or video file that can be downloaded from the Internet, usually focusing on a particular subject area

7   D a webpage featuring a commentary on a particular subject or a journal

2

1   A Girling Hamilton and J Regan Motors in $8 billion merger

2   D US bank pushes for Vietnam infrastructure deals

3   C Haymans and Sons to float

4   B Mixed day for profit announcements (A and D also possible)

5

Unit 17

Getting started

How to live like the idle rich

Understanding

1   A Now is a good time to invest for dividends.

2   B More than £67.8 billion

3   C A minimum of £650,000

4   C We will all effectively have to live off our savings when we retire.

Developing your reading skills

1

1   You should invest across at least 20 stocks to limit your risk.

2   You should invest in international high-yielding stocks that look as though they will sustain good dividend payments.

3   You should also add stocks with more modest yields but good prospects of rapid dividend growth.

2

1   B forecast increase in dividends for next year

2   A the calculation of how much capital must be invested to yield dividends of £26,000

3   B £650,000

4   C living off investments

Language focus

1

1   H short for Financial Times Stock Exchange Index – an index of share prices often used as a measure of business prosperity

2   B the amount produced from an investment

3   D an amount of money held above the minimum level required to counter any risk

4   F another term for salary/wages

5   A shares in the ownership of a company

6   C the level of interest paid on a cash investment

7   E a tax reduction to promote a specific commercial activity or investment

8   G an amount of money available

2

1   irregular

2   strong

3   substantial

4   rapid

5   bumper

6   high-yielding

7   modest

8   looming

3

1   in

2   by

3   of/for

4   off/on

5   on

Review

Answers will vary.

Unit 18

Getting started

Most shares have fallen today.

Understanding

Index	Lost/ gained in points	Lost/ gained in percentage	Closing figure
Dow Jones Industrial Average	-17.10	-0.13%	12,845.13
S&P 500	-0.57	-0.04%	1,344.33
Nasdaq Composite	-3.67	-0.1%	2,901.99

S&P 500 companies saw the smallest fall in share prices.

Developing your reading skills

1

1   Boeing Co.   −1.15%

2   Bank of America Corp.   +1.7%

3   Crude oil   down 93 cents

4   Gold   down $15.40

2

1   Five days

2   12,884.48

3   It has risen by 39.35 points or 0.31%.

4   10,404.49

5   Today, Tuesday

6   $1,724.90

7   Monday

8   $1,712.60

Language focus

1

1   D basic goods that can be traded on the financial markets

2   A another term for stocks or shares

3   F organizations that deal with money, for example, banks and building societies

4   C organizations that discover, develop, and process raw materials, for example metals, chemicals or forestry products

5   G organizations that supply a public service, for example electricity, water or public transport

6   E organizations that make and sell basic consumer products, for example, food, drink, tobacco, prescription drugs and household products

7   H agreements to buy and sell oil at a fixed price at a particular point in the future

8   B agreements to buy and sell gold at a fixed price at a particular point in the future

2

To describe shares going up in value	To describe shares going down in value
advance	decline
gain	fell
rise	retreated
	shed
	slid

3

1   at   3   in   5   on   7   to

2   since   4   to   6   by, at   8   on/in

Unit 19

Getting started

1　A We can improve our own chances of long-term success by learning from Japanese business customs.

2　A Personal business blog

Understanding

1　True

2　False – Japanese companies do welcome suggestions from employees in junior ranks.

3　True

4　False – the mentoring system encourages Japanese businesses to focus on future successes.

5　False – the blogger recommends that people make speeches based on personal knowledge.

6　False – Patricia's comment suggests that she agrees with the main points in the blog.

Developing your reading skills

1

1　E To make an additional point

2　C To show consequence

3　B To provide contrast/balance

4　A To clarify a point

5　D To contrast two different points

2

(Answers will vary. Suggested answer only.)

I'm not so sure about some of the points you make, Danny. The mentoring system is great in theory, but in practice it wastes a lot of time …

Language focus

1

1　D person who writes the blog

2　E place where you can write a comment about the blog

3　A receive or obtain a blog regularly via RSS feed

4　F the blogging community as a whole

5　B web feed format that shows when new content has been added to blogs

6　C software required to view RSS data

2

1　We had several applicants with no particular skill set.

2　A Personal Assistant must have a strong command of multi-tasking.

3　Our work ethic here is heavily influenced by our Australian partners.

4　He is a fountain of knowledge when it comes to blogging.

5　You should take this opportunity to hone your skills.

Review

Answers will vary.

Unit 20

Getting started

4　Books that suggest effective business styles and strategies that can help you improve the way you work.

Understanding

1　A winning company is one that has good leaders who nurture the development of other leaders at all levels of the organization.

2　A leader must teach others to be leaders and build an organization that can sustain its success even when he or she is not around.

3　Ideas, values, and E-cubed (emotional energy and edge).

4　Tichy believes that they should tell stories about their pasts that explain their learning experiences and their beliefs.

5　Yes, Tichy believes that they should show their vulnerabilities in order to serve as effective role models for others

Developing your reading skills

1

1　B different to each other

2　C force, effectiveness

3　A represent

2

1　Disagree

2　Agree

3　Disagree

4　Agree

5　Disagree

Language focus

1

1 encourage
2 develop
3 demonstrate
4 articulate
5 generate

2

1 of
2 of
3 of
4 for
5 as
6 on

3

- use of American vocabulary rather than British vocabulary, for example 'smart' instead of 'clever'.
- use of American spelling, for example, 'behavior' rather than 'behaviour'.

Review

Answers will vary.

This section provides you with information from the COBUILD corpus on key vocabulary items in the units. It gives information on meaning, usage and collocations.

Unit 1 Managing your inbox

urgent/urgently/urgency

- There is an urgent need to address this problem.
- These changes are needed urgently.
- I need you to look at this as a matter of urgency.

COLLOCATIONS
an urgent **need/priority/task/meeting**
urgent **action/attention/talks**
extremely/particularly/increasingly urgent
urgently **need/require** *something*
great/extreme/utmost urgency
a matter/sense/degree of urgency

update

1 noun

- She will give you a brief update on the state of the business.
- Employees receive a daily update of what is happening across the company.
- The software update should solve the problem.

COLLOCATIONS
give/provide/release/issue an update
receive an update
regular/frequent/hourly/daily/weekly updates
a **news/trading** update
a **software** update
an update **on** *something*

2 verb

- We have updated the figures in the table.
- Our anti-virus software needs updating.

COLLOCATIONS
update an **edition/version** of *something*
update **information/software**
update a **list/database**
something **needs** updating
update *something* **regularly/constantly**
update *something* **daily/weekly/annually**
update *something* **automatically**

attach and enclose

1 You use **attach** if you are sending something together with an email.

- Please find a copy of my CV attached.

2 You use **enclose** if you are sending something together with a letter.

- I enclose my completed application form for the post of Administrative Assistant.

address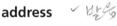

1 noun

If you give an **address**, you make a formal speech in front of a large group of people.

- The CEO gave an address to shareholders.
- The opening address at the conference was delivered by the Managing Director.

COLLOCATIONS
give/deliver an address
an address **to** *someone*
an **opening/closing** address

2 verb

If you **address** a large group of people, you make a formal speech in front of them.

- She will be addressing a meeting of sales representatives later this week.

COLLOCATIONS
address a **meeting/conference**
address an **audience**

review

- Each employee has a one-on-one performance review with his or her boss.
- I'd like you to conduct a detailed review of the department's computer system.
- He's carrying out a review of our pricing policy.

COLLOCATIONS
carry out/conduct/undertake a review
order/demand/seek/require a review
a **weekly/monthly/quarterly/annual** review
a **thorough/comprehensive/detailed** review
a review **of** *something*

Unit 2 Dealing with group emails

external and internal

- Our results have been affected by external factors totally beyond our control.
- A firm of accountants will conduct an external audit of their financial records.

COLLOCATIONS
an external **factor/influence**
an external **debt**
an external **audit**

- An internal memo was sent to all members of staff.
- The company is conducting an internal investigation into the matter.

COLLOCATIONS
an internal **memo/document**
an internal **investigation/inquiry/review**
an internal **audit**

over- and under-

overcharge/undercharge
- He is accused of deliberately overcharging clients.
- Some customers were mistakenly undercharged.

overestimate/underestimate
- We overestimated the size of the market.
- They underestimated the costs involved.

overpayment/underpayment
- The overpayment resulted from a computer error.
- She is owed £1,500 for underpayment over five months.

overvalue/undervalue
- The shares were overvalued.
- The current offer significantly undervalues the company.

mistake and error

1 If you make a **mistake**, you do something that is incorrect.

- This email is full of spelling mistakes.
- The decision proved to be a costly mistake.

COLLOCATIONS
make a mistake
correct/spot a mistake
repeat a mistake
a **serious/grave/terrible/costly** mistake
a **spelling** mistake

2 An **error** is a more formal word for a mistake.
- He made an error when adding up the figures.

- Due to an administrative error, an incorrect payment was made.

COLLOCATIONS
make/commit an error
contain an error
correct/spot an error
a **grave/costly** error
a **technical** error
an **administrative/clerical** error

resolve

- Several fundamental problems have yet to be resolved.
- The issues were fully resolved in discussions with the company.

COLLOCATIONS
resolve a **problem/matter/issue/dispute/crisis**
resolve *something* **quickly/amicably/fully/satisfactorily**

rate

- Interest rates have fallen sharply.
- Investors require higher rates of return from risky companies.
- The country has an amazingly low rate of inflation.

COLLOCATIONS
rate of **return/growth/inflation/interest/commission**
an **interest/exchange/growth/tax/inflation** rate
a **high/low** rate
a rate **rises/increases**
a rate **falls/decreases**
raise/increase a rate
lower/reduce/cut a rate
fix/set a rate

problem/setback/glitch

1 A **problem** is something that causes trouble.
- Technical problems could delay the introduction of new computer disk drives.

2 A **setback** is a problem that stops something from progressing.
- Another delay in production would be a major setback for the firm.

3 A **glitch** is a small problem that stops something from working for a short time.
- Manufacturing glitches have limited the factory's output.

Unit 3 Dealing with long emails

regarding/as regards/with regard to

These three expressions have the same meaning. They are used in formal speech or writing to introduce a particular subject.

- Thank you for your letter regarding the poor service you received.
- As regards the price, this is one of our cheaper products.
- The trade fair proved successful with regard to sales.

defective/faulty/down

1 If something is **defective**, it is not working correctly or has not been made correctly. **Defective** is quite a formal word.

- The company agreed to replace the defective part free of charge.

2 **Faulty** has the same meaning as **defective**, but is a less formal word.

- Many people do not know their rights when it comes to refunds for faulty goods.

3 If a computer system is **down**, it is not working for a temporary period of time. In this sense, **down** is quite an informal word.

- Our Internet is down, so I can't upload anything at the moment.

happen/occur/take place

1 If something **happens**, there is an event, especially one that has not been planned.

- No one can predict exactly what will happen in the markets.

2 **Occur** means the same as **happen**, but is more formal.

- Over 50 percent of the company's sales now occur outside of the United Kingdom.

3 If something **takes place**, there is an event, especially one that has been planned.

- The sales conference took place last week.

refund/reimburse/compensate/credit

1 If you **refund** someone, you give them back the money they have paid you, especially because they have paid too much or they are not happy with goods or services.

- If a customer returns a product because of a quality issue, he or she will be automatically refunded.

2 If you **reimburse** someone, you pay them back money which you have caused them to spend or lose. **Reimburse** is a formal word.

- Your travel expenses for attending the interview will be reimbursed.

3 If you **compensate** someone, you pay them money because they have suffered some kind of loss, damage, or injury.

- The mobile phone company will have to compensate customers for the lack of service.

4 If you **credit** someone, you put money in their bank account.

- We will credit your account by the end of the next working day.

Unit 4 Understanding organizations

experience

- Do you have any experience of working in an office?
- She has gained considerable experience of project management.
- He brings a wealth of experience to the position of Marketing Manager.

COLLOCATIONS
have/bring experience
gain/get experience
previous/relevant experience
practical/hands-on/first-hand/direct experience
considerable/vast experience
a wealth of experience
experience **of/in/with** *something*

expand/diversify/branch out

1 If a business **expands**, it becomes bigger by opening new shops, factories, etc. or by moving into new areas and making more money.
- The business has rapidly expanded and now has stores in more than 23 countries.

2 If a business **diversifies**, it produces a wider range of products or services than before.
- The parent company is diversifying into other industries around the world.

3 If a business **branches out**, it starts to do an activity which it has not done before. **Branch out** is less formal than **diversify**.
- Sky Chefs is branching out into convenience foods.

oversee/supervise

1 If you **oversee** a person or an activity, you are in charge and watch to make sure that things are done correctly.
- Managing partners typically spend over half their time overseeing their firms' day-to-day operations.

2 **Supervise** has the same meaning as **oversee**.
- What are the most common problems when supervising a large project?

chair/preside

1 If you **chair** a meeting or a committee, you are in charge of it.
- He spends much of his time chairing meetings.

2 If you **preside** over a meeting or an activity, you are in charge of it.
- She presided over the merger of the two companies.

presentation

- I was asked to deliver a ten-minute presentation about the project.
- She gave a presentation at a healthcare conference.
- The successful candidate will have excellent presentation skills.

COLLOCATIONS
do/make/give/deliver a presentation
prepare a presentation
attend a presentation
presentation **skills**
a **PowerPoint/multimedia/interactive/ audiovisual** presentation
a **ten-minute/one-hour**, etc. presentation
a **formal** presentation
a presentation **on** *something*

position

- Sue applied for a full-time position as a PA.
- He was offered a senior position in the Marketing Department.
- I am now seeking a managerial position in an engineering firm.

COLLOCATIONS
have/hold/occupy a position
offer *someone* a position
take up/accept a position
a **full-time/part-time** position
a **senior/top/managerial** position
apply for a position

Unit 5 Managing schedules and budgets

forecast

Forecast is used especially when saying what you think will happen in the future based on information which you have now. It can be used as a noun, verb or adjective.

- The company forecast is that third-quarter earnings will be higher.
- It is difficult to forecast what will happen.
- The forecast profit is lower than last year.

task

A **task** is a piece of work which you have to do, especially one that is difficult or unpleasant.

- His first task will be to assess the financial position of the company.

due date/deadline

1 A **due date** is a date on which something should happen. This word is used especially in business contexts.

- Not all customers pay their bills by the due date.

2 A **deadline** is a time or date by which you have to do something.

- The company was forced to employ extra workers to meet the deadline.

revise

- Economic growth forecasts are being revised upwards.
- The June figure was revised from 7.8 per cent reported a month ago.
- The firm may revise its original offer.

COLLOCATIONS
revise *something* **upwards/upward/downwards/downward**
revise *something* **radically/drastically/completely**

revise *something* **extensively/substantially**
revise an **estimate/forecast**
revise a **figure**
revise an **offer/bid**
revise a **version/draft**

delivery

- We guarantee delivery within three working days.
- You can have your goods sent by express delivery for a small charge of only £5.95.
- The suppliers are demanding cash on delivery.

COLLOCATIONS
guarantee/ensure delivery
arrange/arrange for/organize delivery
delay delivery
expect a delivery
take/accept/receive delivery
express/fast/same-day/next-day/overnight delivery
free delivery
on delivery (= when something is delivered)

finalize

- The airline expects to finalize a deal soon to buy engines for its new jets.
- He hopes to have the plan finalized by the end of next year.
- We're finalizing the details of the contract.

COLLOCATIONS
finalize an **agreement/deal/contract**
finalize an **arrangement/plan**
finalize a **merger/buyout/purchase**
finalize **details/paperwork**
finalize **the wording of** *something*

Unit 6 Reading agendas and minutes

attendee/participant

1 An **attendee** is someone who takes part in an event such as a meeting. It is a very formal word used, for example, in the minutes of a business meeting, not in everyday speech.

- All conference attendees will be provided with a map of the university campus.

2 A **participant** is someone who takes part in an event.

- The purpose of the course is to raise participants' awareness of health and safety issues.

apologies

1 In the minutes of a business meeting, there is often a section called *Apologies* which gives the name of anyone who was not able to come to the meeting and the reason for their absence.

- *Apologies*

  Peter Anderson sent apologies because he is away at a sales conference in Portugal.

2 If you send someone your apologies, you say or write something to show that you are sorry.

- Debbie sends her apologies for not answering you, but she is unable to get to her computer at the moment.
- We will offer disappointed customers a refund and our sincere apologies.
- Please accept our apologies for any inconvenience this matter may have caused you.

COLLOCATIONS
send *someone* your apologies
offer *someone* your apologies
accept *someone's* apologies
sincere apologies
unreserved apologies

upcoming/forthcoming/subsequent

1 **Upcoming** describes something that is going to happen soon.

- We have an upcoming sales conference in October.

2 **Forthcoming** has the same meaning as **upcoming**.

- They are very excited about the forthcoming launch of their new range of cosmetics.

3 **Subsequent** describes something happening or coming after something else. It is a formal word.

- The rise in productivity led to the subsequent increase in profit margins.

target

- Senior management of the company has set a target of reducing its distribution costs by 50 per cent within two years.
- The firm has failed to meet targets for sales.

COLLOCATIONS
set a target
meet/achieve/reach/hit a target
exceed a target
agree/define/specify a target
a **sales/budget/growth** target
a **performance** target
an **ambitious** target
a **realistic/achievable** target

SYNONYMS: aim, goal

circulate

- An internal memo was circulated among executives.
- The proposals are contained in a document circulated by the Managing Director.
- Progress reports will be widely circulated.

COLLOCATIONS
circulate an **email/memo/letter**
circulate a **document/copy/draft**
circulate a **leaflet/brochure/pamphlet/flyer**
circulate *something* **widely/nationally/internationally**
circulate *something* **locally/internally**

coordinate

- We must coordinate efforts to deal with the problem.
- It is essential to carefully coordinate the overall marketing strategy.
- He coordinates the activities of all the other departments.

COLLOCATIONS
coordinate **efforts/activities**
coordinate a **response to** *something*
coordinate an **approach/strategy**
coordinate *something* **carefully/closely**
coordinate *something* **effectively**
coordinate **with** *someone/something*

Unit 7 Reading CVs and covering letters

proven

- She has proven business ability.
- We have a proven formula for success.
- The company has a proven track record of innovation.

COLLOCATIONS
a proven **record/track record**
proven **ability/expertise**
a proven **formula**

multi-tasking/multi-task

1 **Multi-tasking** is the ability to do several things at the same time.
- Companies require individuals with multi-tasking skills.
2 If you can **multi-task**, you are able to do several things at the same time.
- He has proved to us that he can multi-task.

promote/promotion

1 If you **promote** someone, you give them a job at a higher level in a company.
- This year I was promoted to Head of Department.
2 If you give someone a **promotion**, you give them a job at a higher level in a company.
- He wants to gain promotion to a senior position.
- She's been singled out for fast-track promotion.
- The chances of promotion within this company are very limited.

COLLOCATIONS
gain/get/earn promotion
deserve promotion
recommend *someone* **for** promotion
give *someone* a promotion
rapid/fast-track promotion
chance(s) of promotion

liaise

- On this project we will have to liaise closely with the IT Department.
- The Account Manager liaises directly with the clients.
- A large part of the job involves liaising between different members of the team.

COLLOCATIONS
liaise **closely/directly**
liaise **regularly/constantly**
liaise **with** *someone/something*
liaise **between** *someone/something*

skill/ability/competency

1 A **skill** is an ability to do something well, especially as a result of a lot of experience and practice.
- What skills and experience can you bring to this job?
2 An **ability** is something you can do well, especially because you are naturally good at it.
- Because of his managerial ability, he was made chairman of the steel company.
3 A **competency** is a skill you need to do a specific job. It is a formal word used in business contexts, for example in a job description.
- The interview will focus on the key competencies required for the post.

referee

- He agreed to act as one of my referees.
- One of your referees should be your most recent employer.
- Consult any people you are thinking of as referees and get their permission first.

COLLOCATIONS
act as a referee
give *someone* **as** a referee
an **academic** referee

Unit 8 Studying job descriptions

performance

- A salesman's performance is measured in terms of the volume of sales.
- Lately the company has improved its financial performance.
- Each employee has a one-on-one performance review with his or her boss.

COLLOCATIONS
measure/evaluate/assess/monitor performance
achieve/deliver/produce a performance
improve/increase/maximize/boost performance
a **good/excellent/strong/outstanding** performance
a **poor/disappointing** performance
economic/financial/business/sales performance
a performance **review/assessment/appraisal**
a performance **indicator/level/measure**

PHRASE
performance-related pay

responsibility

- He will assume additional responsibilities in his new role.
- They offered him a job with managerial responsibility.
- She will have responsibility for operations of the company's Business Information Services division.

COLLOCATIONS
have/carry out a responsibility
accept/assume/take on/face up to a responsibility
meet/fulfil a responsibility
delegate a responsibility
avoid/neglect a responsibility
a **major/heavy/day-to-day** responsibility
a **professional/managerial/financial/departmental** responsibility
a responsibility **for** *something*

result/outcome

1 A **result** is something that happens directly because of something that has happened before.
- You have to give your PR efforts enough time to produce results.

2 An **outcome** is the final result of a process or activity such as a meeting.
- We are not sure what the outcome of the talks will be.

specification

- The original product specification has been amended.
- HR managers will only consider a candidate whose skill set is an exact match for the job specification.
- Turnover is £10m, but the real success lies in consistently meeting customer specifications.

COLLOCATIONS
meet/fulfil/match/comply with a specification
prepare/develop/write a specification
change/alter/amend a specification
a **detailed/exact/precise** specification
a **technical/mechanical/design** specification
a **new/original** specification
a **minimum** specification
a **job/person** specification

requirement

- Electronic products must meet certain essential safety requirements.
- Insurers are required to satisfy various financial requirements.
- We are able to respond quickly and flexibly to customer requirements.

COLLOCATIONS
meet/fulfil/satisfy/comply with a requirement
set/state/specify a requirement
introduce/impose a requirement
remove/dispense with a requirement
a **basic/fundamental** requirement
an **essential/key/compulsory** requirement
a **legal/contractual** requirement
a **formal/official** requirement

PHRASE
surplus to requirements

essential/desirable

1 If something is **essential**, it is completely necessary.
- A degree or equivalent qualification is essential for this role.

2 If something is **desirable**, it would be good to have, but it is not something you absolutely must have.
- Familiarity with database software would be desirable.

Unit 9 Analysing business reports

procedure/process

1 A **procedure** is a way of doing something, especially the correct or normal way.

- What is the procedure for reporting an accident in the workplace?

2 A **process** is a series of actions that have a particular result.

- The manufacturing process is highly automated.

conclusion/finding

1 A **conclusion** is something which you decide is true after considering all the information you have.

- We came to the conclusion that he was not suitable for the job.

2 A **finding** is information which you discover after doing research. This word is often used in its plural form.

- What were the main findings of your research?

recommendation

- He made the recommendations after surveying a group of retailers.
- There will be a financial cost attached to implementing the recommendations in the report.
- She gave him a glowing letter of recommendation.

COLLOCATIONS
make/produce/issue a recommendation
follow/implement/adopt a recommendation
accept/endorse/approve a recommendation
ignore/reject a recommendation
a **specific/detailed** recommendation
a **formal** recommendation
the **main/key** recommendation
a **glowing/enthusiastic** recommendation
on/at someone's recommendation

analysis

- We're conducting an analysis of the trading activity.
- A consultancy was hired to carry out a financial analysis of the firm's operations.
- I was asked to provide a detailed analysis of the sales results.

COLLOCATIONS
do/carry out/conduct/perform an analysis
provide/present an analysis
a **careful/detailed/thorough/in-depth** analysis
a **financial/economic** analysis
a **statistical** analysis
a **cost-benefit/risk** analysis
a **data/content** analysis
an analysis **shows/demonstrates/indicates/reveals** something

market research

- We have carried out extensive market research.
- Larger organizations will have their own market research departments.
- The company also carried out market research into the small-car market.

COLLOCATIONS
do/carry out/conduct/undertake/use market research
a market research **survey/questionnaire**
a market research **department/company/agency**
good-quality/thorough/extensive market research
reliable/serious market research
a **piece of** market research
a **programme of** market research
market research **on/into/about** something

data

- The analysis of all the data isn't due to be completed for some weeks.
- All organizations need to take the protection of customer data with the utmost seriousness.
- US markets focused on economic data showing strong growth in the manufacturing sector.

COLLOCATIONS
collect/gather/obtain data
store/enter data
retrieve/access/analyse/use data
provide/supply data
reliable/accurate data
statistical/economic/technical data
data **collection/storage/analysis/retrieval/processing**
data **protection**
a **piece of** data

Unit 10 Reviewing annual reports

profitable

- The plan is to make this business profitable.
- The company is highly profitable.
- He transformed the loss-making firm into an extremely profitable venture.

COLLOCATIONS
be/become/remain/stay/prove profitable
very/extremely/highly/hugely profitable
barely/marginally profitable
potentially profitable
commercially/financially profitable
a profitable **business/company/enterprise/venture/industry**
profitable **growth**

ANTONYMS
unprofitable, loss-making

in spite of/despite

1 You use **in spite of** to say that something happens even though something else might have prevented it.
- Last year, in spite of the recession, overall French cheese consumption grew.

2 **Despite** has the same meaning as **in spite of**.
- The outlook remains uncertain despite some encouraging recent figures.

cash

- They sold some of their stocks to raise cash.
- She insisted on cash payment.
- He paid for the goods in cash.

COLLOCATIONS
spend/part with/pay cash
earn/generate cash
save/raise cash
need cash
be short of cash/**be strapped for** cash
spare/extra/surplus cash
hard-earned cash
a cash **payment/deposit/withdrawal**
a cash **injection**
cash **flow**

growth

- We have achieved a substantial growth in sales.
- This year, growth is also likely to be strong.
- Interactive telephone services are considered a growth area in the electronics field.

COLLOCATIONS
achieve/show growth
produce/generate growth
encourage/boost/stimulate/accelerate growth
restrict/slow/prevent/inhibit growth
strong/sustained/steady/rapid growth
slow/sluggish growth
economic/monetary/industrial growth
revenue/profit/productivity growth
a growth **area/industry**
a growth **rate**
a growth **in** something

ANTONYM
decline

allocate

- We will allocate some resources for the design stage.
- How should the money be allocated across the various departments?
- Plan your day in blocks and allocate specific lengths of time to certain activities.

COLLOCATIONS
allocate **money/funds/funding**
allocate a **budget/grant**
allocate **resources**
allocate something **fairly/randomly/specifically**
allocate something **to** someone/something
allocate something **for** something

low-risk/high-risk

- Maybe half your investments should be in low-risk funds and trackers.
- Running a restaurant is a high-risk venture.

COLLOCATIONS
a low-risk/high-risk **investment/bond/portfolio**
a low-risk/high-risk **venture/business/project**
a low-risk/high-risk **borrower**
a low-risk/high-risk **strategy/approach**

Unit 11 Browsing advertisements

testimonial/reference/endorsement

1 A **testimonial** is a formal written statement about the qualities of something. Businesses sometimes use testimonials from satisfied customers as part of their advertising.

- Below are testimonials from satisfied clients.

2 A **reference** is a formal written statement about your character and abilities which is written by someone who knows you well or who has worked with you. You often need to provide references when you apply for a job.

- When you are starting your job search, one of the things you will need to consider is who to use for references.

3 An **endorsement** is a statement by a famous or important person in which they recommend a product.

- Companies are paying athletes to Tweet endorsements of products.

be/get caught up in something

If you are **caught up in something**, you have become involved in something, especially something bad.
- The bank was caught up in the implosion of America's subprime market.

potential

- The site offers excellent development potential.
- Setting up your own company can have huge earning potential.
- They recognize the potential which the event has commercially for the city.

COLLOCATIONS
have/provide/show/offer potential
achieve/fulfil/realize *someone's/something's* potential
develop/maximize/exploit *someone's/ something's* potential
someone's/something's **full/maximum** potential
enormous/huge/great/immense/tremendous potential
commercial/earning potential
growth potential

commentary/review

1 A **commentary** is a piece of writing, such as a magazine article, that explains or discusses something.

- He wrote an interesting commentary on the recession in the *Financial Times*.

2 A **review** is an article in a newspaper or magazine that gives an opinion about something such as a new book or film.

- Despite mixed reviews, the film generated $18m in ticket sales in its first three days.

trend

- While the UK's overall retail sector struggled, online sales bucked the trend with strong sales growth.
- She will present a keynote speech that looks at current market trends.
- IT salaries are continuing their downward trend.

COLLOCATIONS
set a trend
follow/continue/reflect/mirror a trend
reverse/halt/buck a trend
an **economic/business/industry/market** trend
a **recent/current/present** trend
a **general/global/worldwide** trend

in-depth

- We have conducted an in-depth financial analysis of the company's operations.
- International companies need people with in-depth knowledge of other cultures.
- The researchers' conclusions are based on an in-depth study of global financial markets.

COLLOCATIONS
an in-depth **study/analysis/investigation/ examination/review**
an in-depth **look at** *something*
in-depth **research**
an in-depth **interview/conversation/discussion**
in-depth **knowledge/understanding**

Unit 12 Product and service brochures

survey

- The firm conducted a survey of customer expectations.
- The survey showed that many companies have revised their equipment investment plans upward.
- A recent survey found that 43% of British respondents own a microwave.

COLLOCATIONS
do/carry out/conduct/a survey
fill in/take part in a survey
a **detailed/comprehensive** survey
a **recent/annual/quarterly/monthly** survey
an **opinion/consumer** survey
a survey **shows/indicates/reveals/suggests/finds** *something*

staggering

If something is **staggering**, it is so great, shocking or surprising that you can hardly believe it.

- The company has announced some staggering sales figures.

ensure/make sure

1 If you **ensure** something, you make certain that it happens. **Ensure** is a formal word that is often used in orders and instructions.

- Please ensure that you arrive at least 15 minutes before the start of the interview.

2 **Make sure** has the same meaning as **ensure**, but is less formal and is used in everyday English.

- We make sure that opportunities for advancement are well known throughout our workforce.

absent/absentee/absenteeism

1 If someone is **absent**, they are not somewhere where they should be, for example at work or at a meeting.

- People may be absent because of sickness or transport problems.

2 An **absentee** is someone who is not present. This is quite a formal word.

- The company had a 10 per cent absentee rate.

3 **Absenteeism** is a situation in which someone is regularly absent from work, especially without good reason.

- High rates of absenteeism might be an indication that a job is being carried out in poor working conditions.

perceive/notice

1 If you **perceive** something, you notice or become aware of it. **Perceive** is a formal word.

- Did you perceive any changes in market trends?

2 If you **notice** something, you are aware that it is there because you can see, hear or feel it.

- I noticed that the number of visits to our website had rapidly increased.

guidance

- Online retailers provide guidance and gift ideas for their customers.
- We are one of the first stock-market advisers to offer minute-by-minute guidance.
- Please could you give me some guidance in terms of pricing?

COLLOCATIONS
give/provide/offer/issue/publish guidance
get/obtain/receive/follow guidance
need/require/seek guidance
practical/useful guidance
detailed/specific/clear guidance
career/vocational/professional guidance

Unit 13 Exploring company websites

access

- The airline might try to gain access to America's huge internal market.
- The bank will have better access to small borrowers.

COLLOCATIONS
have access
get/gain access
give/provide/grant/allow access
deny/block/control/limit access
direct/easy/instant access
free/public/unlimited/unrestricted/open access
Internet/web/online/user access

package

1 A **package** is something that is wrapped or put in a box and sent to someone.
- They sent the package by courier.
2 A **package** is also a set of services that are sold or offered together.
- The company is offering a generous package of employee benefits.
3 A **package** can also mean a set of suggestions or measures for dealing with something.
- The proposal appears in a package of measures to help the aviation industry.
4 In computing, a **package** is a set of computer programs that are sold together.
- We have also developed a word-processing package.

custom/bespoke

1 As an adjective, **custom** describes a product that has been specially made for one particular person. This usage is especially common in American English.
- He makes 150 to 200 custom guitars each year.
2 **Bespoke** has the same meaning as **custom**, but is used in British English especially for clothes and computer software.
- I write bespoke financial software for a global bank.

refund

Refund can be used as a verb or a noun.
1 **Refund** as a verb:
- We regret that we are unable to refund money on tickets once they are booked.
- The airline has offered to refund the cost of the cancelled flights.

COLLOCATIONS
refund *someone's* **money**
refund the **cost of** *something*
refund a **fee/deposit**
refund a **ticket/fare**
refund **the difference**

2 **Refund** as a noun:
- All reputable shops will either exchange the goods or offer a cash refund.
- If there's a long delay in receiving the goods, you can cancel the agreement and get a refund.

COLLOCATIONS
give/offer *someone* a refund
promise/guarantee a refund
ask for/request/demand a refund
claim a refund
get/obtain/receive a refund
a **full/complete/partial** refund
a **tax** refund

words ending in –holder

policyholder
- Policyholders should check their policy details carefully.

bondholder
- The company promised to pay the bondholder $100 a year for every $1000 borrowed.

leaseholder
- A monthly service charge is paid by each of the leaseholders.

shareholder
- This is an important shareholders' meeting.

database

- This firm maintains databases that provide market information.
- Are you getting the most out of your customer database?

COLLOCATIONS
use/search/access a database
build/create a database
maintain/update a database
a **computer/electronic/online** database
a **central/national** database
a **searchable** database
a **large/extensive** database

Unit 14 Social media

hotly/eagerly anticipated

If an event is **hotly** or **eagerly anticipated**, people are excited and pleased that it is going to happen.
- The final countdown to the company's hotly anticipated share flotation began yesterday.

words beginning with pre-

pre-order
- Customers can pre-order the book online.

pre-owned
- The dealership sells both new and pre-owned vehicles.

pre-paid
- A pre-paid envelope is enclosed for your reply.

pre-tax
- Pre-tax profit was £1.6 million.

exclusive

- In addition, you get exclusive access to personal loan and income protection products.
- They agreed to pay the club for the exclusive use of its stadium name.
- The TV company has the exclusive rights to show 60 live Premier League matches a season.

COLLOCATIONS
an exclusive **offer**
exclusive **use/access**
exclusive **rights**
an exclusive **interview/report**
an exclusive **preview/screening**
exclusive **coverage/news**
exclusive **pictures/footage**

sponsor/promoter/backer

1 A **sponsor** is a person or company that pays money to support an event such as a television programme or a sports event, usually in exchange for the right to advertise a product or service at that event.

- The team is looking for corporate sponsors.

2 A **promoter** is someone whose job is to organize and advertise concerts or sports events.
- He is one of Britain's leading boxing promoters.

3 A **backer** is someone who supports a plan or organization, especially by providing money.
- He is struggling to find any financial backers for the venture.

review

- Potential buyers can compare prices and read consumer reviews.
- The film did well at the box office, and the reviews were favourable.
- The magazine includes product reviews and user tips.

COLLOCATIONS
read a review
write/publish a review
a **good/favourable/positive/glowing/rave** review
a **bad/critical/scathing/mixed** review
a **brief/detailed/in-depth** review
a **customer/consumer** review
a **film/movie/book/CD/DVD/restaurant** review
an **online** review

tick all the right boxes

If something **ticks all the right boxes**, it has all the qualities you want it to have.
- As far as retailers are concerned, China ticks all the right boxes.

Tick all the right boxes is an informal idiom. If you want to express the same meaning in a more formal way, you could use the phrase **meet all your requirements**.
- The company responded carefully to our brief, designing a website that met all our requirements.

Unit 15 Reading the news

undermine

- A casual attitude towards deficits would undermine confidence in the euro's stability.
- A strong dollar threatens to undermine international efforts to reduce the U.S. trade deficit.
- Eroding confidence might undermine future economic development.

COLLOCATIONS
undermine someone's **confidence/morale**
undermine someone's **authority/position**
undermine someone's/something's **credibility/integrity/legitimacy**
undermine someone's **trust**
undermine an **effort**
undermine the **stability/foundations of** something
seriously/severely/fatally/completely
undermine something

trigger

- The failure of one bank can trigger the collapse of others.
- If a deal is done, it could trigger a new wave of airline mergers.
- The late delivery triggered a penalty payment.

COLLOCATIONS
trigger **a wave of/a flood of** something
trigger a **response/reaction**
trigger a **protest/backlash**
trigger a **collapse/crisis/panic**
trigger a **debate/discussion/speculation**
trigger a **clause/payment**
trigger something **accidentally/inadvertently**
trigger something **automatically**

crash

- Even after the 1987 stockmarket crash, share prices still gained for the year as a whole.
- Major central banks feared a global recession after the market crash.
- Investors who sold everything after the crash of 1987 lived to regret it.

COLLOCATIONS
a **stockmarket/market/stock** crash
the **1929, 1979**, etc. crash
the crash **of 1929, 1979**, etc.
a **world/global** crash
cause/trigger/contribute to a crash
be hit by/be affected by a crash

predict a crash
the risk/effect/impact of a crash

a gilded age

A **gilded age** is a time in the past when there was a lot of success or happiness.

- The economy, and particularly the rise of industry, produced great prosperity for some whose spending habits gave the period its name – the Gilded Age.

measure

- European monetary authorities may take further measures to defend their currencies.
- The Federal Reserve announced measures aimed at easing strains in money markets.
- A return to profitability will depend on the effectiveness of cost-cutting measures.

COLLOCATIONS
take/introduce/announce/implement/adopt a measure
enforce/impose a measure
approve/pass/support a measure
oppose a measure
a **tough/severe/extreme/drastic/draconian** measure
a **desperate/special/emergency** measure
a **temporary/short-term/interim** measure
a **precautionary/preventative/preventive** measure
an **austerity/cost-cutting** measure
a **safety/security** measure

SYNONYM
step

recession

- The German economy narrowly avoided recession.
- The industry has been hit hard by the global recession.
- Much of East Asia plunged into deep recession.

COLLOCATIONS
go into/enter/suffer a recession
pull something **out of** recession
avoid/survive/weather a recession
a recession **hits** something
a recession **begins/worsens/deepens/bites**
a **deep/severe/prolonged/double dip** recession
a **global/worldwide** recession
an **economic** recession

Unit 16 Business media websites

waive/forfeit

1 If you **waive** something, you officially decide not to demand something even though you have a right to do so.

- Banking bosses are under pressure to waive their bonuses.

2 If you **forfeit** something, you lose a right, benefit or possession because you have broken a law or rule.

- The jury decided that the defendants must forfeit $3.8 million in assets.

bonus/benefit/perk

1 A **bonus** is extra money added to your salary, especially for doing your job well.

- He was paid a bonus of £1,200.

2 A **benefit** is extra money or other things that you get from your employer in addition to your salary, for example a company car or private health insurance.

- The generous benefits package includes medical insurance.

3 A **perk** is a more informal word for a **benefit**.

- As one of the perks of the job, he is given a week's free stay at one of the company's hotels in Spain each year.

go public

If a company decides to **go public**, it offers its shares for sale on the stock exchange.
- Regulators tightly control which companies can go public.

merger

- We are not convinced that the proposed merger will improve services.
- The planned merger was announced to the Stock Exchange.
- Merger talks are taking place.

COLLOCATIONS
propose/discuss/negotiate a merger
agree/approve/complete a merger
announce a merger
block/scupper/oppose a merger
a **possible/potential/proposed/planned** merger

a **failed/aborted** merger
a **bank** merger
a merger **plan/proposal**
a merger **partner**
merger **talks/discussions/negotiations**
a merger **agreement/deal**

infrastructure

- Building the infrastructure alone requires an investment of $20 billion.
- There is little scope to run more trains on the existing infrastructure.
- The Persian Gulf countries will spend perhaps $200 billion on infrastructure projects.

COLLOCATIONS
build/rebuild infrastructure
improve/upgrade/maintain/repair infrastructure
destroy/dismantle infrastructure
basic/key infrastructure
crumbling/decaying/decrepit/dilapidated infrastructure
transport/transportation/rail/ telecommunications infrastructure
infrastructure development/improvement
infrastructure investment/spending/costs

profit

- The company could make a profit of about $57 million on each of the aircraft.
- The bank saw net profit almost double last year.
- Last year, that division had an operating profit of $60.1 million.

COLLOCATIONS
make/earn/generate/deliver/return a profit
announce/report/post/forecast/expect a profit
increase/boost/maximize a profit
a **big/large/huge/massive** profit
a **good/substantial/considerable** profit
a **quick** profit
a **daily/weekly/monthly/yearly** profit
a **half-year/full-year/first**, **second**, etc. **quarter** profit
an **operating/underlying** profit
a **pre-tax/net/gross** profit
profits **rise/increase/grow/soar**
profits **fall/drop**
profits **are up/down**

Unit 17 Analysing the money section

substantial/considerable/bumper

1 You use **substantial** to describe something that is large in amount, importance, size or degree.

- Substantial progress has been made.

2 Considerable is very similar in meaning to **substantial**, but you cannot use it to describe a solid object such as a building.

- There was considerable growth in new jobs.

3 Bumper is a more informal word that you use to describe something that is unusually large.

- She has been offered a bumper pay packet.

loom

If something unpleasant or difficult **looms**, it is likely to happen soon.
- A new downturn in the chemical industry looms.
- There are fears of a looming downturn in business.

yield

- The Eurobanks can offer higher yields on dollar deposits than can U.S. banks.
- Some buyers have been attracted by the 13 per cent dividend yield.
- Increasing yields in the retail sector are coinciding with the falling interest rates.

COLLOCATIONS
produce/offer a yield
increase/improve/maximize/boost a yield
reduce/lower/depress a yield
affect a yield
calculate/determine a yield
a **high** yield
a **low/poor** yield
an **average** yield
a **dividend/bond/rental** yield

credit

- You can get additional sales by extending credit to the biggest and best customers.
- The credit crunch promises more gloom yet for banks.

- The country's poor credit rating makes it unlikely that foreign banks will offer the necessary loans.

COLLOCATIONS
buy/get *something* **on** credit
let *someone* **have** credit
give/offer/extend *someone* credit
get/obtain credit
refuse/deny *someone* credit
interest-free credit
someone's credit **rating/history/record**
a credit **risk**
a credit **limit**
a credit **agreement/facility/arrangement**
a credit **crunch/squeeze**

suspend/postpone/defer

1 If you **suspend** something, you officially stop it for a short time.

- Shipments of the computer were suspended in April.

2 If you **postpone** a planned event, you change its original date or time to a later one.

- The company's annual meeting, twice postponed, is scheduled for 27 September.

3 If you **defer** a decision or action, you delay it until a later date. **Defer** is a formal word.

- The payments can start immediately or be deferred until some later date.

sustain

- The new investment was insufficient to sustain rapid growth.
- The decision reflects confidence in our ability to sustain long-term profitability.
- Can the company sustain a good profit level?

COLLOCATIONS
sustain **growth**
sustain an **economy**
sustain a **relationship**
sustain **momentum**
sustain *something* **financially/economically**
sustain *something* **indefinitely/artificially**

SYNONYM: maintain

Unit 18 Watching the markets

accord

- The two countries have signed a bilateral trade accord.
- The government is negotiating a three-year accord with the IMF.
- The corporation has reached an accord to sell its British oil and gas assets.

COLLOCATIONS
sign/ratify/reach an accord
implement an accord
negotiate an accord
broker/mediate an accord
reject an accord
violate an accord
a **bilateral** accord
a **trade** accord

winning/losing streak

1 A **winning streak** is a period of time during which you have a series of successes.

- The Taiwan stock market halted the two-day winning streak in which it had gathered almost 185 points.

2 A **losing streak** is a period of time during which you have a series of losses.

- The Nikkei Index managed a narrow gain, ending a three-day losing streak.

cut

- The company has announced further job cuts.
- More spending cuts are inevitable.
- The proposed business tax cut hasn't won much applause from either right or left.

COLLOCATIONS
make a cut
announce/propose/demand/impose a cut

oppose/resist/protest against a cut
a **major/massive/drastic** cut
a **spending/public-spending** cut
a **pay/wage** cut
a **tax/capital-gains/interest-rate** cut
a **job** cut
a **price** cut

lose/gain ground

1 If something or someone is **losing ground**, they are becoming increasingly less successful than their competitors.

- The company had a weak July, continuing to lose ground in the car market.

2 If someone or something is **gaining ground**, they are becoming increasingly successful and closer to their competitors.

- The euro is gaining ground on the foreign exchange markets.

commodity

- Coffee beans are the second most valuable traded commodity after crude oil.
- In commodity markets, it is almost impossible to consistently generate above-average returns.
- A futures contract is an agreement to buy or sell a commodity at a set price on a specified date.

COLLOCATIONS
buy/sell/purchase/trade in/trade commodities
export/import a commodity
produce/manufacture a commodity
a **tradable/marketable** commodity
a commodity **price**
a commodity **index/exchange/market**
a commodity **trader/broker**

Unit 19 Reading business blogs

glaringly/blatantly/flagrantly

1 Use **glaringly** to describe a mistake or problem that is very clearly bad or wrong.

- He is concerned about the country's glaringly unfair distribution of wealth.

2 Use **blatantly** if someone does something bad in an obvious way, but they do not show any shame about it.

- It was a ruthless monopoly, blatantly controlled for the profit of a handful of millionaires.

3 Use **flagrantly** if someone does something bad in an obvious way, and they do not care if they break a law or rule.

- The factory owners flagrantly broke safety codes.

innovation

- Direct marketing thrives in companies that encourage innovation.
- Financial market innovation in recent years has been unusually fast.
- Technological innovation is transforming the industry.

COLLOCATIONS
encourage/stimulate/foster/promote innovation
introduce (an) innovation
discourage/stifle/inhibit innovation
(a) **recent** innovation
(an) **exciting/radical** innovation
(a) **marketing/business/financial/managerial** innovation
(a) **technical/technological/high-tech/scientific** innovation
(a) **product** innovation

skill

- Moving large amounts of money requires the skill of professionals.
- The management skills needed to excel at investment banking are different from those in corporate lending.
- Without superior marketing skills, can the group acquire a competitive advantage?

COLLOCATIONS
have/possess/use a skill
learn/acquire/develop/hone a skill
teach a skill
require/need/take skill

great/considerable skill
good/excellent/valuable skills
basic/key/core/advanced skills
practical/analytical/transferable skills
management/leadership/organizational/business skills
technical/computer/IT skills
language/communication skills
social/people/interpersonal skills
someone's skill **set**

prevalent/common

1 If something is **prevalent**, it is very common at a particular time, in a particular place, or among a particular group of people. **Prevalent** is a formal word.

- The most prevalent forecast currently is that the economy will crawl along with modest growth.

2 If something is **common**, it often happens or exists in many places and is not unusual.

- It is extremely common for multinational firms to have divisions in different countries.

kill time

If you **kill time**, you spend time doing a particular activity while waiting for something else.

- To kill some time, he tidied his desk.

enhance

- Electronic media has the potential to greatly enhance communication by companies with shareholders.
- We have increased investment in modern production technology to enhance productivity.
- This is an effective strategy to enhance long-term competitiveness.

COLLOCATIONS
enhance *something* **greatly/enormously/considerably/significantly**
enhance *something* **dramatically**
enhance *something* **technologically/digitally/artificially**
enhance a **reputation**
enhance the **quality/value** of *someone/something*
enhance **performance/productivity/efficiency/effectiveness**
enhance *someone's* **skill/understanding**
enhance *someone's/something's* **prospects**

Unit 20 Reading business books

nurture

- German investors and institutions began nurturing the market rise last year.
- The government is eager to nurture high-tech industries.
- The long-term relationships we nurture have proved advantageous.

COLLOCATIONS
nurture a **skill/talent**
nurture **innovation/creativity**
nurture a **dream/ambition/hope**
nurture a **relationship/friendship**
nurture an **environment**
nurture *something* **carefully/properly/successfully**

express/articulate

1 If you **express** something, you tell or show what you are thinking or feeling by using words or actions.
- Government officials have expressed concern about the levels of debt and foreign influence in recent airline takeovers.
2 If you **articulate** something, you express your thoughts and feelings clearly and effectively.
- Entrepreneurs have got to display a clearly articulated vision for what they want to do.

generate

- The fishery now generates revenue of about $4 million a year.
- The business decided to spend £100,000 on a new machine that will generate a 15% return on its investment.
- The company should actually generate more profit than expected.

COLLOCATIONS
generate **ideas**
generate **discussion/debate/controversy**
generate **interest/excitement/enthusiasm/publicity**
generate **support**
generate **jobs/business**
generate **income/revenue/profits/sales/cash**
generate a **return**
generate **electricity/heat**

decision

- Investment decisions are made by several managers.
- Spain recently took the decision to spend more than $29 billion on improving its rail system.
- The decision was based on economic considerations.

COLLOCATIONS
make/take a decision
reach/come to/arrive at a decision
base a decision **on** *something*
face a decision
delay/postpone a decision
accept/support/uphold a decision
appeal against/challenge a decision
regret a decision
reconsider/review a decision
overturn/overrule/reverse a decision
an **important/big/major/crucial** decision
a **difficult/tough/hard/controversial** decision
an **easy/clear/firm** decision
the **right/wrong** decision
a **good/correct/bad/poor** decision
a **final** decision
a **hasty/snap** decision

emotionally/intellectually

1 **Emotionally** means "in a way that relates to your feelings".
- Entrepreneurs are often too emotionally involved with their inventions to recognize the difficulties of deploying them.
2 **Intellectually** means "in a way that relates to your ability to think and understand".
- She is intellectually superior to the other candidates for the job.

methodology/method

1 A **methodology** is the set of methods and principles which you use when doing a particular kind of work. **Methodology** is a formal word.
- We are developing the methodology to measure and manage core competencies.
2 A **method** is a way of doing something.
- This is the method used by multinational firms to value goods and services bought and sold among subsidiaries.

How should I read? Choosing a reading approach

Every day you read all sorts of different things, from emails to business media websites, annual reports to schedules and budgets. Do you read all these things in the same way? The answer should be no.

Over the next three pages, we will look at different ways of reading *quickly* and reading *carefully*, so that you can match your method to the text. But note that in reality all these methods are linked. For example, you may read through a text quickly to find out the gist before reading it carefully for general understanding. Or you may read a text quickly to find a specific section before reading that section carefully for detail.

Reading quickly

In some situations, you have to be able to read quickly and there are two ways to do this:

1 Reading quickly to get the general idea – skimming

You read in this way when you have limited time but want a general idea of what the text is all about.

Use skimming when reading:

- an extended text for the first time to see if the subject is relevant to you, for example a report, a product/service brochure, or a business blog. If it is, then read it again more carefully.
- an article in a newspaper or magazine or on a business media website to get the gist [an overall understanding] of its meaning.
- a long email to see if it relates to a matter that you need to address urgently.
- a CV or résumé to find out if it is worth taking the time to read more carefully.

Improving your skimming skills

- Choose a text, for example a newspaper article, and set yourself a short time limit, for example two minutes. Read through quickly all the way to the end. Then write a summary sentence about the main point of the article. Reread the article more closely and compare it with your summary sentence.
- Keep your eyes moving forwards. Use a marker to cover up the line you have just read to stop yourself from checking back.
- Do not look up any unknown vocabulary. Try to read it all the way to the end and then look back and see if you really need to look up words to understand the gist of the text.
- If you are really short on time, read just the title, first and last paragraphs, and the topic sentences (the first sentence of each paragraph), which will often be enough to give you the gist of a story.

2 Reading quickly to find specific information – scanning

You read in this way when you have limited time and want to find out something specific in a text.

Use scanning when reading:

- business cards to find specific contact details.
- organigrams to find a particular employee or department.
- job descriptions and CVs/résumés to extract specific information about experience and competencies.
- product/service brochures if you are looking for a particular item.
- websites to find particular information or the correct link.
- the contents page of a report to find the page number of a particular section.
- a newspaper or magazine to find an article that interests you.
- advertisements to see if there is a product/service that you might want to buy.

- social media websites and Twitter to find discussions of interest.
- your inbox to see which emails are marked as urgent.

Improving your scanning skills

- Do not read every word of a text, but train your eyes to pass over the text looking just for the information required. Some people scan paragraphs diagonally or read down the page in the shape of a 'Z'. Find the method that works best for you.
- Practise looking for particular pieces of information in a text – for example, if you are looking for numbers, make your eyes stop at digits; if you're looking for titles, stop when you see capital letters or italics.
- Don't be distracted by information that is not relevant to you. Ignore and skip over these sections of text.
- When you find the piece of information that you require, you may then have to read that section carefully (see below).

Reading carefully

In some situations you need to read a text carefully and there are two ways to do this:

1 Reading extensively for general understanding

You read in this way when you have time and you want a good understanding of what the text is about.

Use this method for reading:

- a newspaper or magazine article in depth.
- a business blog or website that interests you.
- an email.
- business books.

Improving this reading method

- Read as much as you can and whenever you can. The more you read, the easier it becomes.
- Try not to be dependent on a dictionary when reading extensively because this will slow you down. Instead, try to infer the meaning of new words from the context. A useful exercise is to read a chapter of a book without a dictionary and then summarize the main points of it. Then go back and reread the chapter more carefully, looking up unknown words only where necessary. Then look again at your summary to see whether you really needed to use your dictionary to understand the main points of the text.
- See pages 123–124 for tips on improving your speed when reading extensively.

2 Reading intensively to understand every detail

You read in this way when you have time and you need to understand every single detail of the text.

Use this method for reading:

- important business emails, letters, documents, or contracts.
- key sections of business reports or annual reports.
- schedules and budgets.
- job descriptions and CVs of candidates you are interested in.
- agendas and minutes.
- graphs and charts.
- financial and market information.

Improving this reading method

- Use a dictionary when reading for detail.
- If, as part of your job, you regularly need to read the same sorts of documents intensively, focus on learning the vocabulary that is specific to those areas. For example, if you regularly read job descriptions intensively, make sure you understand words that regularly crop up, for example *competencies, responsibilities, outcomes, requirements.*

Don't forget to read the next section **Improving your reading speed** for more tips.

Improving your reading speed

Improving your reading speed is a good challenge to set yourself, but remember that speed is not the most important thing when it comes to reading. There is no point in being able to read quickly if you don't understand what you have read.

However, there are techniques that you can practise that will help you to read more quickly without compromising on understanding. The more you practise, the faster you will read.

Choosing the right texts

It has been shown that people read more quickly when they enjoy what they are reading, so choose what you read very carefully. Make sure that:

- you are interested in what you're reading. Try reading a wide variety of different texts to find subjects you like. If you are interested, then you are more likely to have the motivation to read (quickly) to the end.
- what you are reading is at the right language level for you. If it's too easy, you will get bored and if it's too difficult, you will get lost.

Skim read first

A good way to improve how fast you read is to 'skim' through a text first to work out the gist of what is being said. Pay attention to any headings or charts that might help you. Then when you read the text in detail, you will understand it more quickly than if you were looking at it for the first time, and read faster as a result. Obviously this is not appropriate for longer texts, for example business books, but skimming can be used with shorter texts, for example websites or newspaper articles.

Reading chunks of text

Reading a text is like doing a jigsaw – you must piece together the individual words in order to understand the whole. A jigsaw with lots of small pieces takes much longer to put together than one with just a few large pieces. So, if you can train yourself to read chunks of text (made up of two to five words) at a time rather than reading each word individually, then it won't take you so long to piece together the meaning. For example, when reading, you might group together the following chunks of this extract from Unit 20:

Leaders embody / their teachable points of view / in living stories. / They tell / stories about their pasts / that explain / their learning experiences / and their beliefs.

There are no hard and fast rules for grouping words into chunks and you should find a way that works for you, but you could consider grouping words:

- that are linked by meaning, for example *learning experiences*
- or that are linked by language function – for example, group possessive pronouns with their nouns, for example *their beliefs*, or verbs with their person, for example *Leaders embody.*

Use a pointer

A good way of improving your reading speed is to run your finger or a pen beneath each line of a text as you read. Make sure you keep moving your finger or pen at a regular speed and do not stop to look up unknown words. Do not be tempted to go back and reread sentences because this will slow you down. If necessary, come back and review sentences that you have missed at the end if they have stopped you from understanding the overall meaning of the text. If you find this difficult, use a piece of paper or a ruler to cover up the line you have just read to prevent you from going backwards.

Read in your head

Don't read aloud and don't even move your lips silently when you're reading because this will prevent you from reading any faster than you can speak, even though your brain is capable of taking in information much more quickly than this. However, this is not to say that you should never read aloud because it's a great way to practise your pronunciation and build your confidence. Just remember that it may slow you down. So practise both methods – read in your head when trying to improve your reading speed and read aloud to help your pronunciation.

Focus on the most important words

When reading, some words are more important than others. Concentrate on the words that carry the meaning, for example the nouns, verbs, and adjectives. Pay less attention to the words that hold the sentence together, for example conjunctions, prepositions, or articles. For example, in this sentence you might focus on the words in bold and let your eyes skim over the other words:

Leaders embody their **teachable points** of **view** in **living stories**. They **tell stories** about their **pasts** that **explain** their **learning experiences** and their **beliefs**.

Time yourself and track your progress

A native speaker of English will read an average of 300 words per minute. If you want to find out how many words you read per minute and, more importantly, track your progress at improving your reading speed, then carry out this experiment:

Choose a text from this book and with a stopwatch set yourself a time limit of two minutes to read it. When you have finished, summarize the passage to make sure that you have understood it. Then count the number of words that you have read and divide the number by two to work out how many words you read per minute. Test yourself every few weeks to see if you are getting faster.